Turbulence: Devotionals to steady you through the storms of life

Copyright © 2020 by Matthew Ruttan. All rights reserved. No part of this book may be reproduced in any form or by any electronic or mechanical means, including information storage and retrieval systems, without written permission from the author or publisher, except for the use of brief quotations.

Thicket Books, PO Box 46052 Westdale PO, Winnipeg, MB R3R 3S3

www.thicketbooks.com

Photo of M. Ruttan by Georgia Brieh Photography

Cover design by Roseanna White Designs, RoseannaWhiteDesigns.com

All Scripture quotations, unless otherwise indicated, are taken from the Holy Bible, New International Version®, NIV®. Copyright © 1973, 1978, 1984, 2011 by Biblica, Inc.™ Used by permission of Zondervan. All rights reserved worldwide. www.zondervan.com The "NIV" and "New International Version" are trademarks registered in the United States Patent and Trademark Office by Biblica, Inc.™

Scripture quotations marked NRSV are from the New Revised Standard Version Bible: Anglicized Edition, copyright © 1989, 1995 National Council of the Churches of Christ in the United States of America. Used by permission. All rights reserved.

Scripture quotations marked (NLT) are taken from the Holy Bible, New Living Translation, copyright © 1996, 2004, 2015 by Tyndale House Foundation. Used by permission of Tyndale House Publishers, Inc., Carol Stream, Illinois 60188. All rights reserved.

Scripture quotations marked (ESV) are from the ESV® Bible (The Holy Bible, English Standard Version®), copyright © 2001 by Crossway, a publishing ministry of Good News Publishers. Used by permission. All rights reserved.

Scripture quotations marked CSB have been taken from the Christian Standard Bible®, Copyright © 2017 by Holman Bible Publishers. Used by permission. Christian Standard Bible® and CSB® are federally registered trademarks of Holman Bible Publishers.

CONTENTS

Connect	5
Foreword	11
Turbulence	21
'A Recess Problem' by Sarah Ruttan	160
References and Notes	163
About Matthew Ruttan	167

CONNECT

The "Up!" daily devotional is published five days a week.

Sign up at
www.MatthewRuttan.com/Up
or
www.TheUpDevo.com.

YOU CAN ALSO FOLLOW ON SOCIAL MEDIA:

 facebook.com/MatthewRuttanUp
 twitter.com/theupdevo
 instagram.com/theupdevo

TURBULENCE

Devotionals to steady you through the storms of life

MATTHEW RUTTAN

Thicket Books

I dedicate this book to my mom, Donna, who filled our childhood home with learning, singing, hard work and hugs.

FOREWORD

Ladies and gentlemen, please put on your seatbelts. We're heading into some turbulence.

Life is full of turbulence. When I say "turbulence" I'm talking about the challenges and difficulties that inevitably descend on each and every one of us at some point in this short flight called life. Like the abrupt, knock-you-around blasts of air that seem to randomly attack airplanes, they shake you up and threaten your stability—or even your sanity.

There's an old saying that all humans share two things in common: they're born and they die. My cynical friends add a third category: paying taxes! To that I'll add a fourth: *turbulence*. In fact, I'm guessing you've either been through a storm, are in a storm, or are one phone call away from a storm. And you don't have to live very long to realize that no one gets a free ride.

No one.

A few years ago I was flying to a conference. It was a regular flight out of Pearson International Airport in Toronto. People were putting on seatbelts and choosing which movie to watch on those little screens on the back of the seats. As usual, the pilot's voice came over the intercom system. He started to tell us about things like the weather forecast, how long the flight was going to be, and where the exits were.

And no one was listening.

Maybe that's normal. After all, you've been on flights before and know how la-dee-dah those announcements can seem. But consider the fact that the person who is talking *is the pilot.* He or she is about to launch and navigate your massive aircraft into the sky at insane speeds. We passengers sit there virtually helpless while someone we don't know steers a huge chunk of metal through the clouds. (A huge chunk of metal, I should add, that from a distance resembles a gigantic torpedo.)

As everyone was ignoring the pilot I thought to myself, 'This pilot holds our very lives in his hands—and no one is paying attention to what he is saying!' Some people were looking through those little bags of pretzels and others were trying to untangle their earbuds.

But no one was listening.

The flight to the conference was problem free. But the flight back was another story.

About an hour into the flight—bump, bump! The plane shook—enough for someone to topple over in the centre aisle. A few moments later the pilot's voice came over the intercom. This time he said something that immediately snapped everyone to attention: "Ladies and gentlemen, please put on your seatbelts. We're heading into some turbulence."

People scurried to their seats. If I remember it right, a little light came on, accompanied by a dinging sound. I looked around, and all the same people who were neglecting the pilot's words a short time before were sure listening now!

As I scanned the plane, several people settled into their seats and leaned their heads back with their eyes closed. I thought to myself, 'Huh. I wonder what they're doing.' But then it dawned on me. They were probably praying!

STORMS

As you can probably guess, I'm using the idea of turbulence as a metaphor for the troubles, trials, tribulations and "storms" in life. There are many kinds of storms.

There are family storms where people disagree and there's an all-out feud.

There are relationship storms where communication breaks down, hurtful things are said, and the future teeters on the brink of relational death.

There are health storms where a diagnosis or condition threatens a certain picture of how you thought life was going to unfold for you or for someone you care about.

There are school or career storms where decisions just seem too hard to make and where people or day-to-day environments contaminate your peace of mind.

There are financial storms where the funds dry up and the bills pile up.

There are bad-choice storms where one bad choice (or many bad choices) have rippling consequences for the rest of your life.

There are existential storms when your Plan A dies, or when the things you *thought* you knew fall like a house of cards and you start to question the very meaning of your life.

And there is the COVID-19 storm. But more about that in a minute.

Unfortunately, we often wait until the storms of life descend upon the weather systems of our souls before we proactively tune into the voice of the pilot to know what's going on and what to do next. I say small-p "pilot," but I really mean capital-P Pilot. But I'm guessing you knew that.

As I was thinking through this idea of turbulence and the storms of life, I thought it would be great to speak to an actual pilot to tap into what he or she had to say about the subject. The first pilot I thought about was Amelia Earhart, the first female to fly solo across the Atlantic. Surely she would have some good things to say about navigating turbulence since she was such a bold pioneer of aviation. Then I realized—thanks to Google—that she disappeared in 1937. Oops. I guess she's out.

Then I thought about Leonardo DiCaprio from the movie *Catch Me If You Can*. Then I remembered that (a) he's a celebrity so he will probably never reply to an email from some random guy in Canada; (b) he's an actor and not an actual pilot; and (c) even in the movie he was faking it. Huh. Better keep searching.

Then I remembered that I know a few real flesh-and-blood pilots. One of them is Melissa Mutchler. Our children go to the same school. So I got in touch, explained what I was doing, and asked her this question: "What can you tell me about turbulence? How do pilots deal with it when they come across it?" Here is what she said:

> *Turbulence is a disturbance or irregular motion of the air. It can be caused by other jets (wake turbulence from the vortices of the wing), or by weather patterns such as fronts and thunderstorms. Essentially, they are just rough patches of air. I've experienced lots of turbulence, but very few flights with significantly long distances of rough air.*
>
> *When we are dealing with turbulence we have procedures for the various levels. Obviously, we always try to avoid it. When we do encounter turbulence we turn the seatbelt sign on and ask the passengers to remain seated for safety. In the cockpit, we slow down, ask for reports from other aircrafts through ATC [Air Traffic Control], and try to navigate away from it. Navigating away from it could mean climbing or descending or turning another direction. Sometimes it's not possible. Every situation is different. So we navigate it the best we can, keeping safety and comfort our priority.*

FOREWORD

Thanks so much, Melissa!

In a certain way, I think that we can apply what Melissa said about the turbulence we experience in the air to the turbulence we experience in our souls. We may not like it, and we certainly don't go looking for it, but it happens. Sometimes you can see it coming; sometimes you can't. Sometimes you can steer clear; sometimes you can't. "Every situation is different. So we navigate it the best we can..."

COVID-19

As I write this, our world is in the middle of the COVID-19 pandemic. Things are different. *Very* different. And difficult.

I have family on the other side of the ocean. When I first heard about the coronavirus—whatever it was—it was something they were dealing with *over there*, but it certainly wasn't something we were dealing with *over here*. That changed pretty quickly. The National Hockey League isn't playing games. Television studios aren't making new episodes. School buildings are closed. And our favourite bands aren't touring.

But more importantly, people are sick and dying. Health care and front line workers are making huge sacrifices. People are generally "not okay." Many people have lost their bearings, jobs, money and peace of mind. We can't worship together in the same place on Sundays. Going out for groceries is now a source of anxiety for a lot of people. Children haven't hugged their grandparents, and grandparents haven't hugged their grandchildren. The list goes on. There is an uncertainty which bruises the arrival of each new day—and those of us who live them are tired of having black eyes.

I'm not sure when you'll be reading this. (I'm writing the forward to this book in late May 2020.) Here in Ontario where I live, the curve has been somewhat "flattened." But last week it somehow seemed to un-flatten. It was a reminder that things are probably not going to go back to "normal" as soon as we'd like. Even on the other side of the hump, I don't think anyone doubts the fact that our society—and world—will be different. But in and through it all, there is godly wisdom to steady you through the storms of life. That's what this book is about.

THE "UP!" DEVOTIONAL

Since April 2015 I have written a daily devotional called "Up!" which is published five days a week over email, on various social media platforms, and at www.TheUpDevo.com. It's meant to be read in a minute or less and is designed for daily, down-to-earth discipleship. The topics often include dealing with the challenges in life, what I've here been calling *turbulence*. So I wanted to bring many of these devotionals together in book form for this particularly bumpy season of life's journey. About a third of the entries are from March to May 2020, and the rest are taken from entries over the past few years that I feel are helpful or hopeful for the living of these days.

USE OF SCRIPTURE

Every daily devotional includes at least one quote from the Bible. I think that's important because the Bible is the primary place where we learn about God's will. But a devotional is different from a sermon. A sermon includes sustained study of a biblical passage to uncover some of its meaning and includes an application to daily life in a specific context. But each devotional isn't the result of that kind of sustained study. Some of them are; but the majority are inspired by, or related to, a biblical passage or theme. In either case, I've done my best to be faithful to the spirit of a passage and never misrepresent it. Throughout this book I usually use the New International Version of the Bible, quite simply because it's the version most

English readers have. When I quote another version I make a note of it in brackets.

A BROAD AUDIENCE

Generally speaking, when I write the devotionals I have a broad audience in mind. These are people—probably like you and me—trying to navigate turbulence. Some readers are in their teens, some are seniors, some are in-between. Some are mature Christians, some are new Christians, and some are just curious. Most are in North America, some are in Europe, and some are from who-knows-where. In light of that diversity, I try to get as specific as I can on certain topics, but not so specific that what I say wouldn't apply in a variety of situations. I also tend to include a fair amount of conditional language (i.e. "such-and-such might mean that..."). I do this because each reader is unique and may be in very different circumstances than the next person. Just as I have all this in mind as a writer, I think you should have it in mind as a reader too. So if you are navigating a specific and difficult situation or question, I suggest you do some sustained biblical study, pray, reach out to some wise friends, and speak to your pastor for more guidance.

AWASH IN GRATITUDE

Before we dive in, I want to share some words of gratitude. Thankful people thank people—and I am definitely thankful!

I thank my wife, Laura. She is my other half who is also the better half! She prayerfully supports my ministry, thoughtfully manages our home, and is proactive about her own discipleship. She is still able to make me laugh on a daily basis, challenge me in all the right ways, and offer words of reassurance or encouragement when I'm feeling low. Could I ask for a better wife and best friend? No. No, I could not. Thank you, Jesus.

I thank my children, Sarah, Ben and Anna. They have great questions, boatloads of energy, and a zeal for life that makes me appreciate each new day in a new way. I love watching them grow in their faith, and basking in their light which already shines so brightly.

I thank my mom, Donna. This book is dedicated to her. As I said on the dedication page, she filled our childhood home with learning, singing, hard work and hugs. I appreciate, and have been richly blessed by, her never-failing love through the various chapters of life. Plus, her homemade lasagne is stellar.

I thank my dad, Eric. He died in November 2014. It's amazing how much you can think about someone even when they're not physically with you anymore. His perpetual support, and his honest and unpolished advice, continue to walk alongside me as I grow older.

I thank my brothers, Deric and Jason. We seem to grow closer as the years unfold—not that we were ever *not* close, but you know what I mean. I value their friendship, wisdom, and the laughs we can't help but have whenever we get together.

I thank my wider family circle, from Nashville to Toronto to Woodbridge to Bracebridge (and a few other cities along the way). They ask questions, show their love, have your back, and joke around with the best of them. It's a fortifying gift to have a family circle like this.

I thank my friend Jeff Einboden. He's Presidential Research, Scholarship and Artistry Professor at Northern Illinois University. He has a list of accomplishments as long as the Great Wall of China. But mostly he's a fast friend, confidante, and fellow song-writer who can reify concepts into melodies that both haunt and gladden the heart.

I thank Winston Newman. He's my prayer partner and is one of those people who exudes humility, if that's even possible. His sage counsel, theological acumen, and unceasing prayers have given me direction and encouragement on many a dark day—and some happy ones too.

I thank my feedback writers who I ask to give me occasional pointers about whether or not my writing is clear and makes sense. Sean O'Toole was my high school English Teacher at Bracebridge and Muskoka Lakes Secondary School. Andrew Faiz was the Senior Editor of the Presbyterian Record magazine. Brian Irwin is the Associate Professor of Old Testament/Hebrew Scriptures at Knox College at the University of Toronto. And Jeff Loach is the pastor at St. Paul's Presbyterian Church in Nobleton, Ontario, and is a spiritual director who formerly served as Central Ontario District Director for the Canadian Bible Society. I'm not sure they knew what they were signing up for when they agreed to offer me feedback for a devotional which is now going on five years!—but I continue to benefit from their input.

I thank Lauren Walsh. She diligently chronicles the themes, Bible verses and quotes from each daily devotional. This helps me locate entries and organize my thoughts when putting together various writing projects—including this one. Plus, she's a sunny, intelligent person who is a delight to be around.

I thank Jeff Walther. His ongoing confidence and commitment to the Up! devotional has brought it to thousands of listeners through the Life Radio Network in Central Ontario. His energy and creative thinking for the Gospel is so much fun to be a part of.

I thank the elders, staff, and congregation at Westminster Presbyterian Church in Barrie, Ontario where I've served as the pastor since 2008. Watching them in action through the ups and downs of real-world faith has been a source of inspiration for several of these devotionals. Plus, they've been great supporters of my teaching and writing. The active elders are Cathy Clark, Mary Colvin, Guy Gagnon, Aaron Harris, Wayne Hope, Colin Leonard, Steve Sainsbury, and Tom

FOREWORD

Walsh. The staff is Julie Cunha, Jenn Harris, and Kim Sanderson. Praying, praising and serving alongside one another is an honour that has flavoured my days with lasting contentment.

I thank Matt and Cheryl Brough. They own Thicket Books and have always been enthusiastic and supportive of the Up! devotional. When I asked what they thought about publishing a book of devotionals about navigating *turbulence* they were eager right out of the gate—even with a relatively short timeline.

And I thank *you!* You are the readers. You've bought this book with your hard-earned money or have followed along with the devotional online. Your continued confidence in me is both humbling and motivating. I cherish and celebrate the stories and comments you send in about following Jesus in purposeful, daily ways.

Lastly—and firstly—I thank the Lord. Jesus, standing tall and radiating integrity, is a power unto himself of incomparable magnetism. He is the Living Word I hope to magnify with my written words. May he be glorified today, tomorrow, and while navigating the turbulence of life.

TURBULENCE

FIGHTING FEAR

Fear. It's all around us. And within us. We fear COVID-19. We fear running out of money, time or gas. Some people even fear running out of toilet paper. We fear people who are different. We fear losing, missing out, failure, or not being prepared. We fear criticism, criminals, wrinkles and rain. Oh, and we fear death too. In *The Report Newsmagazine*, Candis McLean reported that "ordinary children today are more fearful than psychiatric patients were in the 1950s."[1] And that was in 2001!

The Bible is full of statements to "not fear." But why? Why *shouldn't* we fear? *Because the powerful presence of God is always more significant than the powerful presence of fear.*

For followers of Jesus, despite what is happening in the world or in our lives, God is always sovereign, he can bring good out of bad, and hope always wins in the end, even if we have challenges to overcome in this short life. What we see isn't all there is to see. Psalm 27:1 captures it well: "The LORD is my light and my salvation—whom shall I fear? The LORD is the stronghold of my life—of whom shall I be afraid?"

I get it. Things like illness, war or famine are concerning. We should pay attention to the authorities, and yes, in the midst of a global pandemic, wash our hands frequently! But mostly, we should pay attention to God. The powerful presence of God is always more significant than the powerful presence of fear.

WHO ARE YOU, REALLY?

In the inspirational movie *Overcomer*, a basketball coach named John Harrison loses his team. Coaching basketball has become such a major part of his identity that it really shakes him. He's also a part of his church's visitation team. In one scene, he visits a man at the hospital. The man asks him who he is. He lists being a coach, a husband, and a white, male, American. Only at the end, when pressed, does he say "Christian." The sick man asks how important that is to him. "Very important," John replies. To that the sick man responds: "Then why is it so far down your list?"[2]

When we forget who we truly are as followers of Jesus, we are more easily shaken and frightened, we seek affirmation in the wrong places, we are quickly influenced by the wrong things, we gravitate toward despair more than hope, are continually searching, and take our eyes off of God.

That's why it's important to not forget John 1:12: "Yet to all who did receive [Jesus], to those who believed in his name, he gave the right to become children of God..." As a follower of Jesus, *that's* who you are. You are a child of God—blessed, loved, chosen, forgiven, adopted, free, saved, powerful, and alive. A true masterpiece! (Just read Ephesians 1-2.)

So if someone asks you who you are—who you *really* are—what would you say? As you face a world that can seem shaky and uncertain, remember that you are a child of God. Because of that unflinching fact, you can live differently, powerfully, and on purpose.

A GREAT CLOUD OF WITNESSES

"Therefore, since we are surrounded by such a great cloud of witnesses, let us throw off everything that hinders and the sin that so easily entangles. And let us run with perseverance the race marked out for us, fixing our eyes on Jesus, the pioneer and perfecter of faith" (Hebrews 12:1-2).

In 1534 Thomas More was imprisoned in the Tower of London. He would be executed by King Henry VIII in July of the following year. Among other things, he used his time in the Tower to write *A Dialogue of Comfort Against Tribulation*. It is a fictional dialogue between two people, Anthony and Vincent. During the conversation, Anthony provides sage and faith-filled wisdom to the younger Vincent.

At one point, Anthony sets the following scene. Imagine that you are walking down a wide street through the middle of a city. On one side there are "a rabble of ragged beggars and madmen" who are calling you names and using all sorts of "villainous words." But along the other side of the street there are "wise and worshipful" people, praising you and cheering you on. And there are fifteen times more of them than there are people who are slandering you on the other side!

Given the situation just described, would you turn back and be totally discouraged by the first group of "mad foolish wretches"? Or would you keep marching forward, head held high, heartened and invigorated by the huge crowd of "that other honourable company"?[3]

You would march forward with your head held high! So do it.

You can't always see them, but in Christ you are "surrounded by such a great cloud of witnesses"—past, present and future. Historically they are called "the communion of saints." They are encouraging you forward in "the race marked out for us."

Don't let the boos of the few distract you from the cheers of the many. Keep fixing your eyes on Jesus, "the pioneer and perfecter of faith," who is the greatest Champion of all.

A CRISIS CREATES CLARITY

A crisis tends to create clarity about what's important. In the wake of Covid-19, many of the things we were previously concerned about are now way down the priority list. We're now dealing with essentials.

And what is essential? Our hope in God. And the people around us. Sure, there are other things. But those are up there, aren't they? Wouldn't it be great if those things stayed at the top of your priority list, no matter what you happened to be going through?

Psalm 39:4-7 says this: "Show me, Lord, my life's end and the number of my days; let me know how fleeting my life is... Everyone is but a breath, even those who seem secure. Surely everyone goes around like a mere phantom; in vain they rush about, heaping up wealth without knowing whose it will finally be. But now, Lord, what do I look for? My hope is in you."

These words are both sobering and focusing. It's never too late. Why not use times of upheaval to re-establish the priorities that matter most?

BLESSED PEOPLE BLESS PEOPLE

A lot of people feel overwhelmed. It's understandable. After all, if you're reading this in 2020 (or maybe even later), there's a pandemic going on. It's easy to feel out of control, uncertain, or even paralyzed. But although you don't have much say about what happens *to* you, you do have a say in what happens *through* you.

God's people can be proactive about seeking and seizing opportunities to bless others. Why? Because *blessed people bless people*. Since God has been so good to us, we share that goodness with others. This is captured perfectly in 1 John 4:11: "Dear friends, since God so loved us, we also ought to love one another."

This could take shape in a variety of ways. It could include picking up groceries for an elderly or sick neighbour, or buying gift cards to support a struggling small business, or taking the time to talk to someone who is overly anxious, or bringing food to a street centre with shelves that are often depleted.

We can't control *everything*, but we can control *some* things. Blessed people bless people.

WITHNESS

Life can be difficult. The only person who hasn't experienced some kind of hardship is the person who hasn't been born yet! Think of Jesus on the cross. He was the only perfect person who ever lived—and even he suffered greatly! None of us are given a free pass in life, but God offers to be with us and help us along the way.

One of the things that makes Psalm 80 special is that it is written in the first person plural. It's a detail that many people miss. Here's what I mean. Verse 19 says, "Restore *us*, Lord

God Almighty; make your face shine on *us*, that *we* may be saved" (emphasis added). We call out to God *together*. We pray *together*. We worship *together*. In fact, it was originally a song put to music, so it would have been something that was also sung *together*. To me it's a subtle reminder that through the hurts of life, we're not alone. Not only is God with us, but we are with other people.

That's why you shouldn't shy away from leaning on others who share your faith. They're the ones you call out to God with, who you pray with, who you worship with, and who you sing with. Can I get a WITHness! (Sorry, couldn't help myself.)

The only person who hasn't experienced some kind of hardship is the person who hasn't been born yet. But for the rest of us, let's not shy away from leaning on others who share our faith. There are times when you might feel alone, but with God and others, you aren't.

WHEN YOU'RE CONFIDENT ABOUT WHAT WILL HAPPEN EVENTUALLY

Let me share an eternal truth that can encourage you: *When you're confident about what will happen eventually, you have more courage for what is happening currently.*

Here's what I mean. When you know that God is eternal, and that one day he is going to make all things new and finally eliminate all mourning and crying and death and pain, it gives you more courage for the difficulties you're currently dealing with. After all, they're temporary.

Imagine a military troop in battle. They're outnumbered and under siege by enemy soldiers. As a result, they're feeling down and out. But then word comes that another one of their units is on the way to provide some big-time backup. In light of this new information, they get a second wind and their hearts inflate with courage! That's what it's like when we know God's big picture plans. We might not know every little detail, but we know that sickness and pain will not last, that strife will give way to peace, and that hope will trample on the head of despair (Revelation 21:1-5). In fact, what happened to Jesus at the resurrection happens to everyone who trusts in him (Ephesians 2:6)! That's why Paul says we can "Be joyful in hope, patient in affliction, faithful in prayer" (Romans 12:12).

Have courage. We've been given a glimpse of the scoreboard at the end of the game of life. Sickness, pain, strife and despair lose. God wins. And you are his. When you're confident about what will happen eventually, you have more courage for what is happening currently.

INTENTIONAL SIMPLICITY

Many of us are living a new version of our own lives. As I write this, air travel is restricted, work and school patterns are shifting, and "physical distancing" is now a real thing. In some (but not all) respects, we are being forced into a simpler way of life —at least, for now.

But did you know that living simply is actually a spiritual discipline? For thousands of years, some Christians have made an intentional effort to de-clutter—both in their minds and in the living of their daily lives—to more fully focus on God, and to more fully enjoy their own existence which had somehow become haggard and frenzied. After months in the arctic, Richard E. Byrd wrote, "I am learning... that a man can live profoundly without masses of things."[4]

In the Bible, Jesus lived simply (and powerfully). He encouraged others to give away possessions or money when they stood in the way of their relationship with God (see Mark

10:21, for example). And In Hebrews 13:5 we read, "Keep your lives free from the love of money and be content with what you have..."

Be content with what you have.

What if, in this chapter of your life, you seized the opportunity to live more simply intentionally? What if you spent less money and more time with God? What if you enjoyed wearing clothes you already have? What if you took a second look at your usual list of activities and crossed out the time-wasters you probably shouldn't have been doing in the first place? Simplicity isn't about less, it's about more. More God, better priorities, more rest, a better joy.

Many of us are living a new version of our own lives. It's different, I know. But what if we used it as a time to clear out the gunk in our mind's eye? Simplicity isn't about less, it's about more.

WHY IS THERE EVIL AND SUFFERING?

Recently someone asked me this: Why is there so much evil and suffering if there is a benevolent being? It's a huge question, perhaps the biggest! And let's be honest. If there was an easy, silver bullet answer, we'd all know it already. You can link to a video of my full response to the question at www.MatthewRuttan.com/videos. But for this devotional, let me just say that *God doesn't promise us freedom from suffering, but to journey with us through it.*

One of the most beautiful and well-known passages about this reality is Psalm 23: "Even though I walk through the valley of the shadow of death, I will fear no evil, for you are with me..." For you are with me. God journeys with us, helps us, and encourages us in a variety of ways—through his Spirit, through worship, through the Bible, through prayer, and also through other people.

Someone was telling me about something horrid they were dealing with. They wondered where God was in the midst of their struggle. In the next sentence they told me about all the helpful people in their life. I told them that I thought God had sent help through those very same people!

Life is hard. Let's not deny it. And there are big questions—some of which we can't easily answer. But even though we sometimes walk through the valley of the shadow of death, we do not need to fear evil, for God is with us.

God doesn't promise us freedom from suffering, but to journey with us through it.

WHEN YOU HAVE SOMETHING GOOD TO LOOK FORWARD TO

When you have something good to look forward to, it softens the blow of what you're currently going through.

We all know it's true. If a child doesn't want to go to school on a Thursday, remind them that the weekend is almost here and it helps. If you're having a tough week, and if you have a fun gathering with friends to look forward to, you're better able to buckle down and get it done. If you have a cast on your arm, and if the cast is coming off in a few weeks, and if your baseball season starts a few weeks after that, the burden of a cast gets a little lighter. Light at the end of the tunnel has a way of shining backward to the one who sees it.

That's the idea behind Paul's thinking in Romans 8: "I consider that our present sufferings are not worth comparing with the glory that will be revealed in us." One day, all of God's creation "will be liberated from its bondage to decay and brought into the freedom and glory of the children of God" (verses 18, 30). He offers a reminder that life's current difficulties are not the end of the story. Sooner or later they will come to an end, all suffering will cease, and glory will be revealed to and in Jesus' followers.

Difficulty is a comma, not a period, in the language of eternity.

So, do you have something good to look forward to? If you're a follower of Jesus, the answer is *Yes*. Remind yourself about God's eternal and amazing promises that are yours. And if you still need some help for your day-to-day life, plan something good—maybe an outing with friends, a Saturday adventure, or a new experience that reminds you who God made you to be.

"I consider that our present sufferings are not worth comparing with the glory that will be revealed in us." When you have something good to look forward to, it softens the blow of what you're currently going through.

BE WHAT YOU WANNA SEE

Be what you wanna see. This statement encourages us to model the attitudes and behaviours that we'd like to see in others.

Let's think about this in terms of how it applies when there is wide public disruption, and even panic, like the COVID-19 pandemic in 2020. What did we want to see? I don't know about you but I wanted to see faithfulness, calm, wisdom and love. Faith instead of fear. Calm instead of panic. Wisdom instead of foolishness. Love instead of apathy.

In Matthew 5:14 and 16, Jesus says this to his followers: "You are the light of the world... let your light shine before others, that they may see your good deeds and glorify your

Father in heaven." Times of widespread public disruption and panic are pretty good times to be the light!

Faith, calm, wisdom and love radiate outward to beat back the darkness that threatens to expand its real estate. Be what you wanna see.

WHEN LIFE FEELS OUT OF CONTROL

We humans like being in control. We're so used to how much we like it, and to how much control we think we have, that we don't even realize it. A simple, modern example is how we can control the temperate of our homes from a smart phone app—even when we're not there!

Previous generations were much more familiar with not having control. They knew what it was to feast or famine based on the weather and crops. Many didn't even have doctors in their towns; illness came often and could be fatal. Fast forward to today. It's easy to think that because we can control *some* things that we should be able to control *all* things. But when certain difficulties come our way—whether that be a dreaded diagnosis, a global pandemic, or losing a job—we are forced to reckon with the fact that some things are in fact simply beyond our control.

So today I'm here to tell you this: *God is in control when you feel out of control.* Psalm 103:19 says, "The LORD has established his throne in heaven, and his kingdom rules over all." In the ancient world, a throne was where a King authoritatively made decisions and cared for subjects. That is what God continues to do today, even if things seem shaky. Are you fearful about something? God is on his throne. Are you finances unsure? God is on his throne. Are you anxious and uncertain about what the future will look like? God is on his throne. And he loves you.

I realize that not having control is hard. But it's important to remember that we never really had it in the first place. We may have had the *illusion* of control, but it was only an illusion. There's an old saying that there are only three days of the week that we have no control over: yesterday, today and tomorrow. The One who really needs to know what he's doing does. What *we* need to do is trust him. God is in control when you feel out of control.

NEGATIVITY IS A TRACTOR BEAM

In the Star Wars movie *A New Hope*, a starship called the Millennium Falcon tries to fly away from a massive space station called the Death Star. It's so big that the young pilot Luke Skywalker first thinks it's a moon. But as they get closer, they realize they can't fly away from it. Captain Han Solo says that a tractor beam is "pulling us in."

I don't know about you, but that's what can easily happen with all the negativity around us. Whether it be news cycles, gossip, or the talk-show talking heads, we can easily get "pulled in." Don't get me wrong. When it comes to being well-informed about world events I'm all for it. But non-stop negativity and friends (in person or online) who love to be doom-and-gloomers can skew our perspective.

In Psalm 103, David intentionally focuses on all the good God has done: "Praise the Lord, my soul, and forget not all his benefits..." (verse 2) He then goes on to list a bunch of those benefits including forgiveness, healing, redemption, love, compassion, and personal renewal. If we are feeling uncertain —and especially *when* we are feeling uncertain—we are wise to remember how God *has* been good to us, how God *is* being good to us, and therefore how God *will* continue to be good to us in the future. God is incredibly consistent like that!

TURBULENCE

Think of your own life. Are you alive? Have you been assured of forgiveness and heaven because of Jesus? Do you have people who love you? Do you have a place to sleep? Do you have some money for food and clothes? Do you have a government with democratically elected officials? Do you have a church home and opportunities to serve? Has God given your life meaning? Do you experience freedom in your country? Do you live in a community with health care, military protection, police, and schools? Wow!

Friends, non-stop negativity is a tractor beam which is powered by our own forgetfulness about God. When we remember how God *has* been good to us, and how God *is* being good to us, we will be more confident about how God *will* continue to be good to us in the future. Today and tomorrow have many good things because God is there.

THE HOUSE STARTED TO SINK

Billy Graham tells a story about a family who purchased a plot of land for a home in the Appalachian Mountains. It was breathtaking, overlooked a valley, and faced some beautiful mountains. They made plans, chose a builder, and the house was completed. After about a year, things started to go terribly wrong. They noticed that the soil was depleted and depressed around the foundation. Cracks started appearing in the walls. A structural engineer discovered that the concrete for the foundation was poured over a pit filled with old stumps, loose rocks, and debris. The house literally started to sink into the ground! Because the foundation wasn't solid.[5]

What is your foundation? Be honest. Because in a solid foundation is... well, foundational to your well-being and hope. Is it your family? Family is nice, but not solid enough. Is it your friends? Friends are nice, but not solid enough. Is it your career? Careers are nice, but not solid enough. Is it your bank account? Money is nice, but not solid enough.

In Ephesians 2:20-21 Paul says that as members of God's household we are "built on the foundation of the apostles and prophets, with Christ Jesus himself as the chief cornerstone. In him the whole building is joined together and rises to become a holy temple in the Lord."

Are you feeling shaky? Uncertain? Like your life is waffling on shifting sand? When we take the foundation out from under a house, it sinks into the ground. But that's not you. Remember your foundation, and even more than that, the "chief cornerstone" whose name is Jesus. And no storm, argument, failure, mistake, uncertainty, or pandemic can body-check him loose. And you are his.

A PURPOSE THAT OFFSETS YOUR PAIN

In Psalm 37 David is feeling frustrated by his lot in life. He feels persecuted and under threat. He has a concern that bad people seem to prosper more than good people. He's angry, and has somehow been hurt or is hurting. But this is what he says: "Do not fret because of those who are evil or be envious of those who do wrong... Trust in the LORD and do good..." (verses 1, 3). Throughout Psalm 37 he stresses that God's people should do good regardless of their circumstances.

We all have hurts and difficulties to deal with. But Psalm 37 is a strong reminder that *a godly purpose in your life can help offset the pain in your life.*[6] David had a strong sense of being called by God for a special purpose. That helped him move forward regardless of his circumstances.

In a similar way, each of us is called by God for a special purpose. And that helps us move forward regardless of our circumstances. If you already know what your godly purpose is, that's great. But for those who are unsure, ask yourself this: "What can I do in this chapter of my life that honours God, and which serves or helps other people?" Write that question down. Or somehow save this devotional. Pray about it. Think about it. If you need some time, set some time aside to think it through some more.

All of us have either been hurt, are hurting, or could hurt at some point in the future. And even though having a godly purpose won't make all your problems go away, it can help focus you on something bigger than your pain; it can renew your perspective. You need a godly purpose in your life to offset the pain in your life.

WHAT YOU'RE DOING IMPACTS HOW YOU'RE DOING

In the previous devotional I highlighted Psalm 37. David was feeling frustrated by his lot in life. He felt persecuted and under threat. He had a concern that bad people seem to prosper more than good people. He was angry, and was somehow hurting. Despite all this, he stressed that God's people should do good regardless of their circumstances. After rhyming off a grocery list of increasing problems, he still summons the wisdom to say, "Hope in the LORD and keep his way" (Psalm 37:34). To me it's a reminder that *what* you're doing impacts *how* you're doing. Here's what I mean.

Quite often, just like David, we feel frustrated, angry or hurting. But we can't let that define us. We need to keep moving forward with God's "way"—his path and agenda. When we do that, it has a positive impact on our perspective. It doesn't mean our hurts will vanish, but it does mean our perspective will improve because we're still focused on doing God's work.

I visited a woman in a nursing home who was frustrated that she couldn't "do as much in the church as she used to." I asked her if she believed in the power of prayer. "Of course," she replied. So I asked her to pray morning and night for the church's programs, its people, and our community. She agreed. A few months later she told me she was doing it. Did it make all her problems go away? No. But she felt better about having a more specific godly purpose.

Friends, hurt is a part of life—but it doesn't need to be the defining part. "Hope in the LORD and keep his way." *What* you're doing impacts *how* you're doing.

THE STRENGTHENING EFFECT OF PRAISING GOD

Do you want to be fortified, braced, strengthened? Me too. That's why it's vital to *praise God*. Here's how those things are connected.

In Psalm 103 David talks about praising God. A lot. Check it out: Verse 1: "Praise the LORD, my soul; all my inmost being, praise his holy name." Verse 2: "Praise the LORD, my soul…" Verse 20: "Praise the LORD…" Verse 21: "Praise the LORD…" Verse 22: "Praise the LORD… Praise the LORD, my soul." That's a lot!

When we think of praising God we usually think about celebrating God in a formal worship setting. That definitely makes sense. But on a more day-to-day basis, we can also think of it as *speaking well of who God is and the good God does*. When we do that it fortifies, braces and strengthens us. Why? Because we are reminded that despite our changing times, we belong to the God who does not change; and that when there is so much bad news, we have a good God who gives many good things; and that when our society is spinning with dizziness, we are firmly directed by the compassionate commands of our comforting King.

No matter where we are we can praise God. This includes Sunday morning worship services, on live-streamed services online, with faith-at-home resources, but also in our daily attitudes and conversations. Speak well of who God is and the good God does. Looking up in praise plants our feet firmly on the ground.

HOW WILL WE JUDGE OURSELVES?

Why do bad things happen? Well, in certain situations that's an easy question to answer. For example, if we drive carelessly and hurt ourselves in an accident the reason is because we were driving carelessly. But there are other times when an explanation isn't so easy. But do you know what? Even when we don't know *why* certain things happen, we know *what* to do: *Love God and help one another.* As Jesus says in Luke 6:31: "Do to others as you would have them do to you." The golden rule is golden for a reason: It's very valuable to those who receive help!

There's a grocery store cashier who, in light of the coronavirus pandemic, now thinks of her job more clearly as a significant way to serve others. Someone I know asked that people donate money to a struggling street centre as a way to mark their birthday. Someone else makes a praying gesture with their hands when they see police or firefighters drive by, as if to say "thank you" and "I'm praying for you." Someone else frequently earmarks time in their schedule to call and check in on people who might be lonely.

Sometime in the future, when we look back on our lives, how will we judge our actions? Will we look in the mirror and judge ourselves based on whether we were able to philosophically or existentially explain everything that was going on in our lives? Probably not. My guess is that we'll judge ourselves based on whether or not we loved God and helped one another.

Even when we don't know *why* certain things happen, we know *what* to do. Love God and help one another.

CALMING DOWN

Worry. It happens. We turn on the news and witness a non-stop litany of bad news. Plus, we have a tendency to hear all the doom and gloom and silently rehearse worst-case-scenarios in our heads over and over again. That's why it's important to relax. To calm down. Panic is a breeding ground for knee-jerk reactions, not thoughtful and faithful decisions, about how to live.

There's a story about some people who brought a woman who was caught in adultery to Jesus. They wanted to stone her because that's what the law of Moses allowed. They wanted to know what Jesus thought about it. Jesus didn't respond right away. "Jesus bent down and started to write on the ground with his finger" (John 8:6). What in the world was he doing? One of my seminary professors had a theory: Jesus was taking time to think before he responded. He was taking a moment to compose himself. Only then do we hear his famous words: "Let any one of you who is without sin be the first to throw a stone at her" (verse 7). The text doesn't actually tell us why Jesus did what he did. But pausing to think before we react is great counsel for all of us.

In the ongoing effort to calm your mind in a world of bad news, worst case scenarios and non-stop notifications, and as you try to think and act from a place of greater balance, maybe you should develop some habits that help you do just that.

Maybe you could not check your phone for the hour before you go to bed. Or what about journaling, or going for a walk, or turning off the news and surfing over to that channel with the live fire place!—unless, of course, you have an *actual* fireplace.

I don't know what's going on in your life right now. But maybe you have a lot of worry and stress. That's why being intentional about relaxing your mind is so important. Panic is a breeding ground for knee-jerk reactions, not thoughtful and faithful decisions, about how to live. "Calm down" is something we usually say to someone else. But sometimes you also need to say it to yourself.

THE WEAPON OF PRAYER

A lot of people are fighting a war with fear. Fear of illness or unemployment or loneliness or... the list goes on. So in these next several devotionals I'm going to highlight several weapons in the war against fear. They're not *physical* weapons, but *spiritual* weapons.

The first is prayer. Simply put, prayer is conversation with God. In the book of Hebrews, we learn that because of Christ, who is our "great high priest," we can "approach God's throne of grace with confidence, so that we may receive mercy and find grace to help us in our time of need" (Hebrews 4:14, 16). We can talk with the powerful Creator of the universe, not because we're moral superstars who deserve to be heard (we're not and we don't), but because our perfect and loving Saviour Jesus has given us an all-access backstage pass to the very throne room of God!

One of the reasons this is so significant is because *fear feeds on the idea that there is no one to help you.* But there is. Not only does prayer more intimately connect you to God through conversation, but it makes an actual difference! We may not always understand how God acts, but he does. The great Swiss theologian Karl Barth put it like this: God "is not deaf, he listens and, moreover he acts. He does not act in the same way whether we pray or not. Prayer has an influence on the action, on the very existence, of God."[7]

So take the time and take up a weapon—and pray. Because of Christ, who is our "great high priest," we can confidently "approach God's throne of grace with confidence, so that we may receive mercy and find grace to help us in our time of need."

FEAR FEEDS ON FORGETFULNESS

This week I'm highlighting several weapons in the war against fear. They're not *physical* weapons, but *spiritual* weapons. Some people are afraid of getting sick, or a loss of income, or the unknown—the list goes on.

Yesterday I wrote about the weapon of prayer. Today is about *memorizing and meditating on Scripture*. Let me explain why I consider that a weapon. In the Bible, Joshua was told to "meditate" on the "Book of the Law... so that you may be careful to do everything written in it" (Joshua 1:8). In Psalm 119, the psalmist frequently spoke of meditating on Scripture, as in verse 15: "I will meditate on your precepts and fix my eyes on your ways." This can be done through reading, but also through memorization. It's about pondering, thinking deeply, and internalizing. It's embedding God's word in your mind with the goal of filling yourself with a more intimate knowledge of his word and wisdom.

Why does this make a difference? *Because fear feeds on forgetfulness about God.* When you're feeling unsure, fear sees an opening and pounces. He wants you to forget who God is, how good God is, and the powerful things God can do. But if you've embedded God's word and wisdom into your mind, you can recall it at a moment's notice and preach fear back down to size!

Imagine awaiting test results, or that you're about to go into one of those huge M.R.I. machines. Fear sees an opening and pounces. But you recognize what is going on and beat it back with Psalm 23:4: "Even though I walk through the darkest valley, I will fear no evil, for you are with me..." Or what if you start to doubt your purpose. Or what if you're susceptible to criticizing lies about who you are and what you can accomplish in life. But you recognize what is going on and beat it back with Ephesians 2:10: "For we are God's handiwork, created in Christ Jesus to do good works..."

If you think memorization is intimidating start small. One verse per week, and build from there. Look up some powerful Bible verses and write them down in a special place to memorize. Fear feeds on forgetfulness about God. So don't forget. Embed God's word in your mind and heart to preach fear back down to size.

THE SWORD OF THE SPIRIT

I sometimes hear struggling Christians say that they know the Bible is important, but that they don't read it as much as they should. Here's some motivation. The Bible is a weapon in the war against fear. Why? *Because fear feeds on uncertainty and untruth.*

When we're going through something challenging, our brains are working overtime and in over-drive, making up worst case scenarios, and jumbling our thoughts about who we are, who to trust, and what our priorities should be. But in Ephesians 6:17, a well-known passage about God's people being ready for spiritual warfare, Paul writes: "Take the helmet of salvation and the sword of the Spirit, which is the word of God." God's written word to us—the Bible—is a part of this weaponry: the "sword of the Spirit."

In these uncertain times, how do you know the difference between a need God will provide, and a want? How do you know what your number-one parenting priority should be? How do you learn to be more content, or to have more peace, or to be the person God wants you to be, regardless of what's happening in life? In short, we read the Bible, and ask for God to increase our understanding.

Read it every day. If you're already doing that, awesome. Keep it up. If not, start with Matthew, Mark, Luke or John. You'll be encouraged to know that Jesus' disciples didn't always understand everything either. But they were so captivated by him that they wanted more! And so will you.

As a result, you'll be better equipped to think and act from a place of faith instead of fear—firmly rooted in God's wisdom —instead of just reacting to the noisy cultural buzz which is bombarding us 24/7. Arm yourself. "Take the helmet of salvation and the sword of the Spirit, which is the word of God."

HIS POWER AT WORK WITHIN US

In these past few devotionals I've been highlighting some tools you can use in the war against fear, whether it be fear of the unknown, illness, or financial problems. But I'm calling them weapons. These aren't *physical* weapons, but *spiritual* ones. There are many weapons we could use. But here I'm highlighting what I think we can pick up and brandish quickly.

Today's weapon is "acts of service." It's about helping or serving others. Here's why it matters in the war against fear: *Fear feeds on you feeling useless*. It senses when you feel para-

TURBULENCE

lyzed by how big something is, and pounces on how small you feel. But guess what. You're not.

First of all, what Paul says in Ephesians 2:10 applies to followers of Jesus today too: "For we are God's handiwork, created in Christ Jesus to do good works..." Second, when you serve others as the hands and feet of Jesus, *God can work through you*. As Paul says later in Ephesians 3:20: "Now to him who is able to do immeasurably more than all we ask or imagine, according to his power that is at work within us..."

His power that is at work within us.

Mark Batterson tells a story about his friend Joel who was serving at a church in South Africa and feeling particularly "low" in his faith. One night he went to McDonalds with just enough money to buy a Happy Meal. But he noticed some street kids in the parking lot and felt God prompting him to buy them some burgers. So he bought five junior cheeseburgers. But by the time he went over to the kids, the group had doubled in size! He thought about cutting the burgers in half so they would each get some. But as he started handing them out, they just kept on coming! There was enough for every kid to get a burger. And then, at the bottom, there was even one left for him. Did McDonalds make a "mistake"? Or did God sizzle up some extras when Joel started to serve?[8]

One of the things I've discovered is that *when you serve others you often see a Servant Saviour at work*. Not only does it honour God and help others, but it beats back the fear who loves feeding on your feelings of uselessness. "Now to him who is able to do immeasurably more than all we ask or imagine, according to his power that is at work within us..."

HIS POWER AT WORK WITHIN US

In a society that celebrates volume, vanity and rivalry, it is tempting to just think that it's all up to us, and that when things go well in our lives, that it must be the result of our own strength and unparalleled intelligence. But Paul models a different attitude. In Philippians 4:13 he writes, "I can do all this *through him who gives me strength*" (emphasis added).

It's important to note that this isn't a blanket statement about Christ's strength for whatever you happen to be doing. It's about relying on *his* strength for contentment while serving *him*. Paul is content *while serving God*. He doesn't expect that God is going to make him content or give him strength if he's just working through his own selfish agenda. He clearly lives *for God's glory*.

But why is this so hard? Partly because we live in a consumer culture that says you need to get contentment from outside sources—from having cool stuff, from being successful in the eyes of others, and from always having great weekend experiences that make it appear like you're having the time of your life on Instagram.

Pastor Jud Wilhite highlights how backward this is: "Contentment isn't sustained from the outside in, but from the inside out."[9] That's why your internal life is so important—that's your personal relationship with God, cultivated with Bible reading, with prayer, with rest, with quieting your mind and giving thanks to God for all the ways he has been working in your life and providing good things.

When we do the work God wants us to do, and when we focus on him and not the million other lesser distractions, he will give us strength for that work, and we will learn to be content, like Paul. Never give up relying on Christ's strength—not yours—for contentment in Christ's service. Nurture the relationship. "Contentment isn't sustained from the outside in, but from the inside out."

WHAT YOU EXPOSE YOURSELF TO

Christian Keysers has an article about "mirror neurons" in a book called *What's Next? Dispatches on the Future of Science*. He's a super-smart guy with a Ph.D. in neuroscience. In it he highlights findings about how our brains operate.

Do you ever feel happy when you see someone else laugh? Or hurt when someone's in pain? Or how about feeling hungry when you see someone gobbling down your favourite snack? A part of the reason we feel impacted in these ways is because of how our brains operate. What we take in through our senses impacts us. The neurons that fire in our own brains when we see and hear someone else laugh are the same ones that fire when we laugh. The mind and body have a way of knowing it's not really us doing it, but the same neurons are working in us when we see those actions in others. Think of the implications. When we see violence and negativity all the time, our brains are partially functioning as if we were participating in those things ourselves. Alternatively, when we proactively expose ourselves to good and godly things, our brains fire as if we are participating in those things ourselves.

Keysers actually quotes Jesus in Matthew 7:12 when thinking through the implications: "do to others what you would have them do to you..." Our brains seem to be "intuitively predisposed... to this maxim,"[10] Keysers writes.

Friends, think through how you fill your brain. What you expose yourself to shapes you. So choose well.

FEAR DOESN'T DEFINE US

The crucifixion and resurrection of Jesus are the main event in the Christian faith. I've always been struck by how the women were described as they stood outside the empty tomb on that first Easter morning: "So the women hurried away from the tomb, afraid yet filled with joy, and ran to tell his disciples" (Matthew 28:8).

Afraid yet filled with joy.

Maybe they were afraid because they had seen and experienced a lot, including the torture and cruel death of their friend and leader. They had seen an earthquake, an angel, and rugged, well-armed guards. Yet at the same time they were filled with joy. They learned Jesus was alive again—and they were about to see him personally a few seconds later. Here's the thing. *Fear may be inside us, but it doesn't define us.* For them. And for you.

There was a young boy being treated for leukemia. Someone referred to him as a cancer patient. In response he said, "I may be a cancer patient, but I'm *more* than a cancer patient too; I am a child of God." He had cancer, but he refused to let it define him.

Do you have fear? It's okay to admit it. It's good to be honest. But it doesn't need to define you. As followers of a risen Redeemer, we are defined by him. Fear may be inside us, but it doesn't define us.

IN A WORLD WHERE RESURRECTION IS POSSIBLE

The resurrection is central to Christian faith. Paul says that if Jesus has not been raised then your faith is "useless" (1 Corinthians 15:14). It changes how we see and experience the world. Why? *Because in a world where resurrection is possible, anything is possible!* The New Testament writers continually highlight that our world and lives are exploding with new possibilities because of what happened to Jesus. In Romans 6:5 Paul writes: "We were therefore buried with him through baptism into death in order that, just as Christ was raised from the dead through the glory of the Father, we too may live a new life."

But it's just so easy to get sucked in to the cynicism of our times that nothing can change, that death always wins, and that hope is a perpetually popped balloon. But in a world where resurrection is possible, anything is possible. Lives are changed all the time—powerfully. People give and live sacrificially for the benefit of others; enemies are loved; healing occurs; miracles happen; and the laughter of a child can change a hardened heart forever.

We are an Easter people, even if it's not technically Easter. God is powerful and in charge and with us. Which world do you live in? Because in a world where resurrection is possible, anything is possible.

JOY HAS A JOB TO DO

Joy has a job to do. Let me explain. Imagine seeing Jesus crucified—and then alive again! The disciples did. Talk about an emotional roller coaster. And what did Jesus tell them to do afterward? To get in touch with their feelings for ten years and then come back for some instructions when they're feeling all warm and cozy inside? Nope. He gathered his disciples and told them to go make more disciples: "All authority in heaven and on earth has been given to me. Therefore go and make disciples of all nations, baptizing them in the name of the Father and of the Son and of the Holy Spirit, and teaching them to obey everything I have commanded you. And surely I am with you always, to the very end of the age" (Matthew 28:18-20).

That's what I mean when I say that joy has a job to do. Resurrection joy doesn't hide; it spreads. Being and sharing Jesus' love, truth and hope with others is definitely being faithful to his words, but there's a side benefit too. It makes you more content. After all, you feel useful to God and a blessing to others!

It will involve prayer. It will involve knowledge about Jesus' teachings. And it may involve a variety of other things, including providing for someone's physical, mental or spiritual needs, or demonstrating the daily difference hope makes. But one thing's for sure. Joy doesn't sit on its hands. Joy has a job to do. Therefore, so do you.

IMPERFECT

After his resurrection, Jesus gave his followers the great commission: to make disciples of all people (see Matthew 28:18-20). But just before he did that, we're told something very telling: "When they saw him, they worshiped him; but some doubted" (Matthew 28:17). Some worshiped Jesus—*but some doubted!* But he tells the group to make disciples anyway. In other words, this world-changing mandate wasn't just given to those who had it all figured out. He also gave it to those who were still struggling with what they had seen and experienced.

What does this mean for us today? It means that *perfection is not a necessary qualification for being a disciple or for making disciples.* When it comes to serving God, you need to know who the Truth is not what all the answers are. Or, put another way, it's about knowing Someone not knowing everything. Just like those first disciples. You aren't required to be able to quote from every book in the Bible, or have a snappy answer to why bad things sometimes happen to good people, or have a perfect track record of loving your neighbour. You need to know Jesus.

Do you use your own imperfection as an excuse? You shouldn't. None of us have it all figured out, including me. Being a disciple, and making other disciples, isn't about how awesome *you* are, but how awesome *he* is. Perfection is not a necessary qualification.

THE RIGHTEOUS FOR THE REBEL

In the book of Isaiah there are four "servant songs" which include prophecies about a future Messiah who is also a servant who suffers on behalf of his people. This Messiah and servant is Jesus.

Isaiah 53:12 (CSB) says that "he bore the sin of many and interceded for the rebels." At first glance, this seems to be about the two criminals who were crucified alongside Jesus (Luke 23:32). But isn't it also about you and me? Maybe "rebels" seems like too harsh a description. I realize that we are made the image of God (Genesis 1:27), that we are "fearfully and wonderfully made" (Psalm 139:14), and that we are "God's handiwork, created in Christ Jesus to do good works" (Ephesians 2:10). But we also rebel against God and his commands. Isaiah 53:6 describes us well: "We all, like sheep, have gone astray, each of us has turned to our own way..."

And what happened? Did he let us go? No. Jesus the Righteous One gave his life for ours, the rebellious ones. This isn't to make you feel bad about how bad you are, but good about how good God is! Makes you thankful, doesn't it?

Do you get discouraged by your bad days? By your mistakes, sin or selfishness? Me too. The good news is that you're not forever defined by your rebellion; you're forever defined by a Redeemer. No one is too far gone for God's reach. Including you.

DON'T BEAT YOURSELF UP

Today I'm here to tell you to cut yourself some slack. Here's why. As I write this, we're living through a global pandemic. Has buying groceries ever been this complicated? More people are working from home (or adjusting to a new work situation), homeschooling their kids, trying to think through extracurricular (if even possible), dealing with limited access to services that previously provided care and support, and trying to stay in touch with loved ones. Some are fighting the challenges of isolation or anxiety. The list goes on.

Well, guess what? You can't do it all. And I don't think you should try. You'll just be perpetually disappointed. You're not a bad person for not being able to "have it all together." We are living through a global pandemic for goodness sake! Did you miss some homeschooling? Don't beat yourself up. Did you [insert-your-own-personal-disappointment-here]? You're not Godzilla.

I love what Jesus said in Matthew 11:28: "Come to me, all you who are weary and burdened, and I will give you rest." Jesus is our rest. Our standing and peace with God is based on what Jesus has done, not what we have done—or haven't done. And during times like these I find great solace in that—in the embrace, strength and peace that only he provides. Maybe you can to.

Times are tough. Things are different. Fix your eyes on God. And cut yourself some slack. Our righteousness, rest and reason for hope is Christ.

CHRIST CANNOT BE QUARANTINED

Where is God in a pandemic? It's a big question. But in this devotional let me just say two things. First, God is always on his throne. Nothing ever changes that. He is our sovereign and eternal ruler and king. Second, God is in *you* and working through *you*!

In John 15:4 Jesus said to his disciples, "Abide in me, and I in you." In 2 Corinthians 13:5 (ESV), Paul asks the Corinthians, "Or do you not realize this about yourselves, that Jesus Christ is in you?" That's huge!

I once heard a story about a boy who was asked, "Who is a saint?" Quite innocently, the boy replied, "A saint is someone the sun shines through." Someone had told him that the people in the stained-glass windows at church were called saints. The sun "shone through" them. It works on a deeper level too. In the New Testament, a "saint" is simply an everyday person who has a special purpose as a follower of Jesus. In this way, a saint is definitely "someone the Son shines through." That's you.

Where is God, even in a pandemic? As always he is on his throne, and he is living in and working through his people. God is on the move more than you might think. Christ cannot be quarantined.

IN YOUR PAIN

In the first century, one of the reasons many people rejected the idea that Jesus was the Messiah was because he suffered and experienced pain. We humans can often think that the presence of pain means the absence of God—back then or now. Some people continue to think that suffering—whether it be at the hands of a global virus, or at the hands of a crazed gunman—must mean that God isn't near.

But Jesus is the greatest and most perfect example not only of God being with us, but being with us distinctly *in our pain*, and experiencing pain *with* us.

Dietrich Bonhoeffer was a German theologian, professor and pastor who was imprisoned in World War Two for his opposition to Adolf Hitler. In a letter from prison in July 1944 he wrote that "only a suffering God can help."[11] In his book *Where is God in a Coronavirus World?*, Professor John Lennox writes: "a Christian is not so much a person who has solved the problem of pain, suffering and the coronavirus, but one who has come to love and trust a God who has himself suffered."[12]

We worship and serve a God who knows what it's like to suffer, and who is with us and helps us through that very experience of suffering. In Romans 8:26 Paul writes: "the Spirit helps us in our weakness. We do not know what we ought to pray for, but the Spirit himself intercedes for us through wordless groans."

God is not in an ivory tower above the clouds twiddling his thumbs. He is walking along side us—strengthening us and guiding us—with his own wounds and tears. *The presence of pain does not mean the absence of God.* And in fact, "only a suffering God can help." God is with us in our hardship, helping us through it, and drawing our eyes to a hope-filled day when all suffering will be a distant memory.

YOUR MENTAL HEALTH—NOW MORE THAN EVER

The phrase "mental health" doesn't come up in the Bible. But that doesn't mean God isn't interested in our mental health.

God loves and cares about us, and that clearly includes our minds.

The Bible is full of stories about people who struggled. Job, David and Paul come to mind. Psalm 88 ends like this: "You have taken from me friend and neighbor—darkness is my closest friend" (verse 18). When you think darkness is your closest friend you are definitely going through something bad!

My gut tells me that, in light of COVID-19, most people are currently experiencing more mental strain than they think they are, and certainly more than they're used to. Symptoms might be materializing now. Some won't show up until later. It's hard to be sure. Either way—and I'm just speculating here—but we may be standing on the threshold of a mental health epidemic of epic proportions. *What is clear is that you need to be proactive—not just reactive—about your mental health.*

I'm not a psychotherapist; I'm a pastor. And from my vantage point we need to limit non-stop news (we can't mentally sustain panic-mode indefinitely), get a decent amount of rest, get our bodies moving, be mindful of our diet, adopt a healthy approach to social media, cut ourselves some slack once in a while, and reach out to trusted friends and lean on each other. But most of all we need to fix our eyes on Jesus like never before. There is no enduring answer or peace outside of him. Ever.

One of the many encouraging and comforting words we receive in the Bible is in Psalm 34:18: "The Lord is close to the brokenhearted and saves those who are crushed in spirit." Be proactive (not just reactive) about your mental health.

SHOUTS IN OUR PAIN

What I'm about to say might be difficult to hear. But *God can grow you through what you go through.* Even when it's difficult.

In Romans, Paul explains that when we are given eternal peace with God through Christ, it changes our perspective about everything else. "And we boast in the hope of the glory of God. Not only so, but we also glory in our sufferings, because we know that suffering produces perseverance; perseverance, character; and character, hope" (Romans 5:2-4). Suffering, then perseverance, then character, and then hope!

C.S. Lewis is known as a best-selling author and world-class literary critic. He also faced his fair share of hardship. His mother died when he was young; he fought in World War One; was wounded in that same war; and had to bury his wife. In a book called *The Problem of Pain*, he wrote: "Pain insists upon being attended to. God whispers to us in our pleasures, speaks in our conscience, but shouts in our pain: it is His megaphone to rouse a deaf world."[13] What I think Lewis is saying is that pain is so powerful that it gets our attention; it wakes us up to hear what God might be saying to us with greater clarity. That doesn't mean that pain and hardship are good. But *God can grow you through what you go through*. Even when it's difficult.

Are you experiencing some sort of hardship? I'm guessing yes. Ask yourself: How might God be trying to grow me through this experience—to make me wiser, stronger, more humble, more loving, or more faithful? God can grow you through what you go through. Are you listening for his voice?

ONLY 15 FEET AT A TIME

There's an old saying for travelers: The headlights in your car only light up the road in front of you 15 feet at a time—but those fifteen feet will get you all the way to your destination. When you think about it, it's profound. Miles and miles of darkness stretch out before you. You need light on every inch of that road to navigate the journey successfully. But even though your headlights only give you fifteen feet at a time, those fifteen feet will guide you all the way to your destination.

That's like the road of life. And God. We *want* to know what's ahead. We *want* to have certainty about the future. We *want* to have clarity about what's around the corner. But God gives us light for fifteen feet at the time. And with him as the source of that light, it's all we really need. Psalm 119:105 says it clearly: "Your word is a lamp to my feet; and a light to my path." Fifteen feet at a time.

Do you feel like you're wandering into darkness or uncertainty? Do you crave to know what's ahead? To have certainty about your future? Fifteen feet is all you truly need. The Lord leads us all the way, but he does it day by day.

A TIME TO RE-EVALUATE SUCCESS

What if you had a faulty understanding of success? If so, you'd probably have the wrong goals. And each day you'd probably miss the mark.

In Deuteronomy 8:2 Moses was speaking to the Hebrews after they had wandered through the wilderness for forty years: "Remember how the LORD your God led you all the way in the wilderness these forty years, to humble and test you in order to know what was in your heart, whether or not you would keep his commands." As they journeyed through the wilderness, "success" was *daily, humble faithfulness*. It was about living each day trusting that God was who he said he was, and that he would do what he said he was going to do. It included humility—because they needed to trust that God was in charge (not them), and also the faith to keep his commands.

That continues to be a great understanding of success: *daily, humble faithfulness*. As we wander into an uncertain future, things will continue to evolve, and our directions will most likely shift. Plan A will become Plan B, and then Plan C... and eventually Plan J! But we are less likely to be disappointed and more likely to keep our eyes fixed on our eternal and gracious God if we have a better understanding of what it means to be successful in the first place.

At the end each day we can measure our mettle with questions like: 'Did I honour God today?' and 'Did I care for others today?' Those are goals worth shooting for—no matter what life throws your way. Success is daily, humble faithfulness.

LIFE A LIFE-SUSTAINING FEAST—OR AN OCCASIONAL SNACK?

In yesterday's devotional I said that times like these are a good time to re-evaluate our understanding of success. Today I'm going to encourage us to re-evaluate the role of the Bible in our lives.

Moses reminded the ancient Hebrews that God was a God who kept his word. That's why he fed them manna: "to teach you that man does not live on bread alone but on every word that comes from the mouth of the LORD" (Deuteronomy 8:3). Jesus himself quoted that same verse when he was tempted by Satan in Matthew 4:4. Think of that for a second. If you don't have food, you die. If you don't have air, you die. And if you don't have God's word and will—you die!

So seek God's word and will as if they were as essential to your well-being as food or air. I realize that we live in a world that values physical things and de-values spiritual things. We obsess about our physical health but easily dismiss our spiritual health. But when it comes to the big picture, physical death can be bad, but spiritual death is way worse!

Do you treat God's word and will in your life like the life-sustaining feast it is? Or like an occasional snack? Seek God's word and will as if they were as essential to your well-being as food or air. Because they are.

VIRTUE STANDETH

People are motivated by different things. Some people feel motivated to do something if they know they'll get a nice reward at the end. Others are motivated if they know they are doing something that will make someone feel good. Today I want to appeal to those who (a) are experiencing difficulty, and (b) are motivated by a challenge.

In 1534 Thomas More wrote a book called *A Dialogue of Comfort Against Tribulation* while imprisoned in the Tower of London. It was the year before his execution by King Henry VIII. In it, a character named Anthony says this: "For, as the philosophers said very well of old, 'virtue standeth in things of hardness and difficulty.'"[14]

Virtue standeth in things of hardness and difficulty.

That got me thinking about true virtue—about moral strength and goodness—and about how it can remain unbudging through "hardness and difficulty." There's the challenge: to continue in moral strength and goodness (virtue) even in difficulty. I don't know what the 'philosophers of old' had in mind, but when it comes to God's people, our moral strength and goodness come from Jesus. As he himself said in John 14:6, he is "the way and the truth and the life..."

I realize that when you're going through "hardness and difficulty" you're not always at your best. Neither am I! But by the grace of God, we can try to live with virtue as we look to the leadership and muscle of Christ. It can be a part of our devotion to God, and it can also be a source of strength to the people we care about—people who are probably also struggling, and who might need someone reliable to lean on (like you).

Let's be fortified for the challenge by these words from the apostle Peter to the elders in 1 Peter 5:10: "And the God of all grace, who called you to his eternal glory in Christ, after you have suffered a little while, will himself restore you and make you strong, firm and steadfast. To him be the power for ever and ever. Amen."

BRAINS LIKE A BROKEN ETCH-A-SKETCH?

What will next month hold? Or next year? Or the next five years? Truth is, we're just not sure. But guess what? God provides.

Speaking to the Hebrews in Deuteronomy 8:4, Moses reminded them about this very fact, even as they had wandered through the wilderness for forty years: "Your clothes did no wear out and your feet did not swell during these forty years." They needed the reminder because it was so easy to forget that God provides—even when there's uncertainty about what tomorrow will bring.

The same is true for us. Worry can be a symptom of forgetfulness. I remember shopping at a thrift store and finding an Etch-A-Sketch. Remember those? They were those red-framed drawing contraptions. You turned the knobs to draw something. To erase your drawing, you had to flip it upside down and shake it. But this one would erase automatically after a few seconds. You didn't even have to shake it. That's like our own forgetfulness when it comes to God. Quite often, the day isn't even over before and we've automatically forgotten everything he's done for us! Do you have eternal peace with God through Christ? Some food in the fridge?

Clothes to wear? A church to call home? A friend to talk to? Wi-Fi?

God provides—even as you journey into an uncertain future which you don't know much about. Today, pay attention. When you notice the good God *has* done for you it builds confidence about what he will *continue* to do for you.

THIS CHAPTER ISN'T YOUR FINAL CHAPTER

Let me go out on a limb for a moment. Your life isn't totally ideal right now. Am I right? I get it. A global pandemic isn't really a fun factory. That's why I'm here to tell you some good news: *The current chapter of your story isn't the final chapter of your story.*

Hardship. Will. Pass. It's the reason Paul can say this: "Therefore we do not lose heart. Though outwardly we are wasting away, yet inwardly we are being renewed day by day. For our light and momentary troubles are achieving for us an eternal glory that far outweighs them all. So we fix our eyes not on what is seen, but on what is unseen, since what is seen is temporary, but what is unseen is eternal" (2 Corinthians 4:16-18).

When I was young I remember my parents driving me to a hockey tournament in America. (I live in Canada.) I was so excited. I got to play hockey, stay in a hotel with a pool, and go to McDonald's all in one weekend! But after we crossed the border, the first neighbourhood we saw was really rough. Some of the windows in the houses were boarded over and there were potholes in the streets. "Are we there?" I asked. "Nope, just passing through." I was so glad for that answer! Our destination was still an hour down the road and was going to be waayyy better!

And so is ours. We're just passing through these trials.

They're temporary. Our destination is going to be waayyy better! The current chapter of your story isn't the final chapter of your story. Hold fast. Persevere. "For our light and momentary troubles are achieving for us an eternal glory that far outweighs them all. So we fix our eyes not on what is seen, but on what is unseen, since what is seen is temporary, but what is unseen is eternal."

NO MATTER WHAT

I want to share a word of grace in a difficult time. Something I've noticed is that many people are being really hard on themselves. I get it. You want to do well. You want to put your best foot forward in every area of your life. You want to hit the proverbial ball out of the park. But then something unexpected comes along and throws you off track, or you get behind, or you have a bad day (or month) and become overly self-critical.

So I just want to tell you that God continues to love you—even when you get thrown off track, or get behind, or have a bad day (or month) and become overly self-critical. Should we try to do God's will? Should we try to be at our best, not only for God, but for ourselves and for the people around us? Absolutely. But you are valued in God's sight not because of how successful you are, but because of *whose* you are. As we are reminded in Psalm 103:13: "As a father has compassion on his children, so the Lord has compassion on those who fear him..." Heavenly Father. Children. Family. Unconditional love.

As today rolls forward... inhale... exhale... smile... pray... feel the embrace of a father who has compassion his children, including you. As John Ortberg says: "The reason I don't have to prove my worth is that I am loved by God no matter what."[15]

REMEMBER THIS FEELING

Recently I came across a picture that someone from my congregation posted on Instagram in winter. It was snowy and she was cross-country skiing to church! It's a picture that is both beautiful and powerful in its simplicity.

It got me thinking about the things we take for granted—like going to a worship service with other flesh-and-blood people. Like going out and grabbing a bite to eat with friends. Like hugs. Like school functions. Like concerts. Like sports. Like zipping in and out of whatever store we want. Like family gatherings. It made me so grateful for all the things we take for granted.

Do you want to know what worries me? That when social-distancing restrictions start to ease, we will forget what this feels like, that we will quickly start to take everything for granted—again. But it doesn't need to be that way. In Ephesians 5:19-20 Paul gave this advice: "Sing and make music from your heart to the Lord, always giving thanks to God the Father for everything, in the name of our Lord Jesus Christ." Always giving thanks to God the Father *for everything*.

Remember this feeling. And let this strange time in human history re-open our eyes to the million gifts we so often enjoy but don't even notice because they don't have a bow.

THE RIGHT ATTITUDE

I once heard about a man who had a heart attack. His life flashed before his eyes which scared him. As a result, he started to take better care of himself, pay more attention to the people he cared about, and live by better priorities.

A friend noticed the change and came to visit. "How'd you like your heart attack?" he asked. "Not very much," the man replied. "Really? Since it happened, you've started to take better care of yourself, pay more attention to the people you care about, and are living by better priorities! So let me ask you again: How'd you like your heart attack?" "Well, when you put it like that, I guess it liked it pretty good!" It's a story about perspective. The heart attack wasn't good. But when the man looked at the positive change it brought into his life, he saw it in a new light.

In James 1:2-3, Jesus' half-brother offers this challenging but perspective-shifting advice: "Consider it pure joy, my brothers and sisters, whenever you face trials of many kinds, because you know that the testing of your faith produces perseverance." If we're open to seeing things in a new way—the trials we face, and the tests to our faith—we start to perceive how God forties us for the rigors of life with greater perseverance and steadfastness.

Resilient people adopt the right attitude. As a result, they also adopt the right *altitude* for navigating the problems they face. We may not be able to change the things that have happened to us. But we can change how we look at them.

LUKEWARM OR LOYAL?

In the Bible, the word "love" is close to what we mean today when we talk about "loyalty." To *love* God is to be *loyal* to the God who made us, saves us, provides for us, and guides us no matter what we're going through.

Consider Shadrach, Meshach and Abednego. In Daniel 3 they were told to worship the false gods of the powerful King

Nebuchadnezzar. If they didn't do it, they would be thrown into a blazing furnace! A. Blazing. Furnace! Here's what they said: "If we are thrown into the blazing furnace, the God we serve is able to deliver us from it, and he will deliver us from Your Majesty's hand. But even if he does not, we want you to know, Your Majesty, that we will not serve your gods..." (verses 17-18). Wow. *That* is loyalty. *That* is love.

What does going through hardship reveal about your faith? Are you loyal to God no matter what? Or does it make you realize that you're a fair-weathered follower? If you stand strong, heart rooted in a powerful and hope-filled Redeemer, that's awesome. If not, it's never too late to drain your heart of lukewarm "faith" and fill it with a firm loyalty to our never-failing God.

Resilient people are loyal to God not matter what—the God who will prove to be loyal to them throughout this life, and into the next.

THE TRIANGLE OF DISCERNMENT

Have you ever asked God for sign? After all, life overflows with difficult decisions, ambiguous pathways, and sundry uncertainties. That's why asking God for some kind of clarity or confirmation can be so enticing. There's good news: God has already given us direction about how to clarify his will for our lives. Let me suggest three methods in what I call the "triangle of discernment."

The first point on the triangle is the Bible. It's the primary place where we learn about God's will. 2 Timothy 3:16 says that all Scripture is "inspired." That's huge! It's pregnant and giving birth to God's wisdom every day. The second point on the triangle is prayer. If I listed all of the places in the Bible where we are encouraged to pray and talk with God this post would be twenty pages long. The third point on the triangle is counsel. This is simply getting together with other trustworthy Christians to talk through your situation, question or problem, and getting their input. 1 Corinthians 12 describes the church as a "body" where everyone has different gifts to share with the group; two of those gifts are wisdom and knowledge. I also think of Proverbs 15:22: "Plans fail for lack of counsel, but with many advisors they succeed."

Do you need direction from God? Try the triangle of discernment: Bible, prayer and counsel. God's wisdom might be more accessible—and obtainable—than you think.

A LICENSE PLATE OR A MESSAGE FROM GOD?

Frederick Buechner was upset about his daughter's illness. If you've ever worried about a sick child maybe you can relate to that gut-wrenching reality. He was sitting at the side of the road parked in his car depressed and afraid. All of a sudden, another car came up from behind him as if out of nowhere and passed by. He looked up and noticed that it had a personalized license plate with a single word. Buechner says it was "the one word out of all the words in the dictionary that I needed most to see exactly then."

TRUST

He chose to understand it as a message from God.[16]

Was it biblical? Check. Perhaps a response to prayer? Check. An encouraging word to lift the head and heart while stumbling through the uncertain shadows of life, family and illness? Check. Psalm 56:3-4 (NLT) says, "when I am afraid, I will put my trust in you. I praise God for what he has promised. I trust in God, so why should I be afraid?"

I think God is communicating with us all the time.

Through the Bible, through prayer, through the wisdom of other godly people, through worship—and through everyday moments we can too easily write off as "coincidence." Why wouldn't he? He loves you like a precious, priceless child because you *are* his precious, priceless child.

What if God is proactively reaching out to you with a word of encouragement, wisdom or direction? Are you paying enough attention to notice?

MOMENTS THAT TONE THE MUSCLE OF YOUR CHARACTER

Jonathan Haidt is a psychologist who did a hypothetical experiment. People were given a summary of the life story of a girl named Jillian. Here are some of the details. At a young age, Jillian developed a learning disability which would delay her ability to read, and which impacted her grades and work throughout life. In high school she would become best friends Megan who would get cancer and pass away. She would also get hit by a drunk driver. Although not her fault, a boy would die in the accident which sent her into a depression. She would go to a state school and get a job. She would eventually lose her job when the economy tanked. She would have to move from her house to an apartment, and would forever struggle to make ends meet.

The participants were then asked to imagine that Jillian was their own daughter. But she hasn't been born yet. They were then told they could have five minutes to edit her story to change how her life would unfold.[17] What would they do? A lot of people would immediately take out the hardships. After all, we want our loved ones to be healthy and happy all the time, right? But what if it was our hardships which made us more resilient? What if Jillian learned how to persevere through life *because* of her many hardships?

I'm not saying that hardships are good. But unlike Haidt's experiment, they're not something we can simply edit out of our lives because we don't like them. They key for us is to be deliberate about not letting our hardships define us. Instead, we can think of them as moments which tone the muscle of our character.

Are you going down? No! Are you defeated? No! Are you despairing? No! Are you done? No! Alternatively, are you going to persevere? Yes! Are you going to win? Yes! Are you going to choose hope? Yes! Are you going to be resilient in the footsteps of Jesus? Yes!

"Blessed is the one who perseveres under trial because, having stood the test, that person will receive the crown of life that the Lord has promised to those who love him" (James 1:12).

MEANING IN THE MINUTIA

The great artist Michelangelo painted the Sistine Chapel's ceiling in the Vatican. It took several years and included four hundred figures and nine scenes! A friend noticed all the details Michelangelo was putting into the corners of the chapel ceiling—corners that were incredibly far away and therefore difficult for the naked eye to see. "No one will ever see them," he said. In response Michelangelo replied, "God will."[18]

Do you think no one sees, notices, or appreciates all the faithful work you do? In your house, at the office, with your family, in a special project, or at school?

God does.

In Ecclesiastes 3:13, the writer observes how people can "find satisfaction in all their toil," and that this is "the gift of

God." Since we can understand our daily work as a gift from God, it motivates and encourages us because he's the one we're primarily doing it for!

That's why *there is meaning in the minutia.* It's an expression coined by my wife, Laura. There is meaning in the minutia because as we think, live and work, we do so with the brains, muscles and hearts given to us by Almighty God himself.

Do you think no one sees, notices, or appreciates all the faithful work you do? In your house, at the office, with your family, in a special project, or at school? Not so fast. God does. And he's the one who matters most.

THE BATTLE OF THE MIND

The battle many people are fighting right now is the battle of the mind. Franticness. Failure. Fear. Loneliness. Loss. Lethargy. Distress. Disappointment. Doubt. So how do you win the battle of the mind?

In 2 Corinthians 10:5 Paul writes: "We demolish arguments and every pretension that sets itself up against the knowledge of God, and we take captive every thought to make it obedient to Christ." Great advice! "Take captive every thought to make it obedient to Christ."

If a thought comes into your head that says, 'You have every reason to fear!' Respond by saying, 'I trust in Christ.' If a thought comes into your head that says, 'You're not going to make it!' Respond by saying, 'I trust in Christ.' If a thought comes into your head that says, 'You're such a failure!' Respond by saying, 'I trust in Christ.'

Friends, if you're a follower of Jesus, you're not even the main warrior in your own battle—He is! And he can—and does—slay the enemy of truth. As we are reminded in that great hymn, A Mighty Fortress is Our God: "One little word shall fell him."[19]

Take captive every thought to make it obedient to Christ.

THE PRUDENT GIVE THOUGHT TO THEIR… CLICKS

When life feels crazy, there's a way to be proactive about your well-being which is easily neglect. It's to *adopt a realistic approach to social media*.

Here's why it's important. A lot of people are on social media. Some of it they like; but a lot of it they don't. Why is that? My guess is that we can be naïve about the 'realistic-ness' of what we're seeing. Then we compare our lives to other people's lives—which aren't necessarily what they appear to be! We see someone having non-stop, laughter-saturated family time—and don't see the other six days of the week when they're literally tearing their hair out. We see someone with perfect skin—and forget that they're using a filter. We see someone doing cool project after cool project—and don't realize that they're wildly unfulfilled in their personal life. Plus, a lot of people post comments or share links—sometimes negative—without that sober second thought about whether or not it's the wise thing to do.

Perhaps Proverbs 14:15 is in order: "The simple believe anything, but the prudent give thought to their steps." I think that the prudent give thought to their clicks and social media use as well. Adopt a realistic approach to social media.

NOT SOME CHEAP SUBSTITUTE

I recently read that the real reason the Titanic sank wasn't because it hit an iceberg. Well, sure, that's the main reason, but it wasn't the only reason. Apparently, there was a shortage of good quality bolts when it was being built. So the builders settled for cheap rivets as replacements. Rivets held the steel plates together in the ship. So when the Titanic hit the iceberg, the cheap rivets popped their heads, leading to the ship's demise.[20]

Well, my friends, the good news is that in this uncertain season of life—this uncertain storm—*God* is the one who is holding us together, not some cheap substitute!

Don't settle for a short-term, Band-Aid solution to your longing for help and hope. We follow and worship Someone whose truth is more certain than any talking head on T.V., whose love is longer-lasting than any relationship you could ever have on earth, and whose hand is more healing than any pill, medicine or surgery.

In John 8: 12 Jesus said: "I am the light of the world. Whoever follows me will never walk in darkness, but will have the light of life." *The* light of the world. Never walk in darkness. Will have the light of life.

Look to the One—and walk alongside the One—who offers light through the fog, strength for the storm, mercy in the meltdowns, and provision for the future. The winds may be blowing, but remember this: In this uncertain season of life—this uncertain storm—we are held together not by some cheap substitute, but by the Lord of eternity.

THE MOMENTS YOU ALREADY HAVE

Things are different. Including your routines. As a result, your spiritual habits have probably taken a hit. Do you find it harder to carve out time to read the Bible, or pray, or worship, or connect with your small group, or do family devotions, or serve others, or _____? If so, you're not alone.

In May 2020 I had a great online conversation with two colleagues and friends—Alex Douglas and Christine O'Reilly. [You can watch the full conversation at www.MatthewRuttan.com.] Something Alex talked about was this challenge that many people are experiencing. But just because the opportunities to grow in our faith are strained or different, that doesn't mean they aren't there. We *can seize the moments we already have*—whatever they might be—to grow in faith. This applies for individuals, couples or families.

Maybe you can't do your usual volunteering, whether that be at the youth centre or in the Sunday morning kids' or music ministry—but you can probably get to know or help your neighbours. Maybe your child can't go to a summer Bible camp —but you can talk about the promises and power of God on your morning walk. Get what I'm saying?

In James 2:26 we learn that "faith without deeds is dead." Too often, we think the "deeds of faith" are official programs or events organized by somebody else. But more often than not, the deeds of faith are daily expressions of our faith in Christ even when we don't know what those days will bring. Just because the opportunities to grow in our faith are strained or different, that doesn't mean they aren't there. Seize the moments you already have.

INDEPENDENT OR INTER-DEPENDENT?

Something a lot of people want to be is independent—not having to rely on other people for anything. It goes along with being "self-made" or "self-reliant." But one of the things COVID-19 has taught us is how *inter*-dependent we are.

This point was made in a conversation I had with a friend and colleague named Christine O'Reilly. Speaking about COVID-19, she said: "This has taught us how interdependent we are... upon a lot of people that we might not normally take the time to acknowledge." It's so true. We are seeing, with increasing clarity, the value of people who stock the shelves at the grocery store, or who deliver packages, or who do hundreds of other valuable jobs we might not normally acknowledge.

We might think we're independent, autonomous people. But we're not. We're inter-dependent, social people. And this should compel us to have a more humble, compassionate and loving attitude toward the people around us. They make important contributions to our lives and society—even if we don't always think about them.

In Romans 12, Paul writes: "Love must be sincere. Hate what is evil; cling to what is good. Be devoted to one another in love. Honor one another above yourselves... Share with the Lord's people who are in need. Practice hospitality" (verses 10, 13).

I believe we're more likely to have this kind of attitude (a) when we remember that in Christ we belong to God and he has done so much more for us than we could ever do for ourselves, and (b) when we truly value each child of God in the living of our interconnected lives.

"This has taught us how interdependent we are... upon a lot of people that we might not normally take the time to acknowledge." So acknowledge them. Value them. And let's love one another with eyes wide open to the many ways we are enriched on a daily basis by people we often don't even see.

A MERCIFUL RESET

In an article for *The Gospel Coalition Canada* called "Better Than Before," Darryl Dash quotes a prayer that was once handed to a pastor: "Pray that God uses these days as a merciful reset of our lives."[21] What a powerful perspective and prayer for us as well. That these days—as difficult and uncertain as they are—can be a "merciful reset" of our lives.

Is there something in your life that needs re-setting? Some priorities? Your relationship with God? Something else? What if *now* was the time to hit reset?

It's the perfect time. After all, things have changed and continue to change. You've probably already learned to adapt to various situations and demands—and more quickly than before. My guess is that you're thinking about (or are more open to) the big questions of life—even in the busyness or loneliness of your days.

In Psalm 138:7-8 David writes: "Though I walk in the midst of trouble, you preserve my life. You stretch out your hand against the anger of my foes... do not abandon the works of your hands." David asks God to preserve his life... because he is the work of God's very hands! That goes for us as well. 'Heavenly Father, preserve our lives! We too are the work of your hands! What do we need to change? We are open to what you want to do in and through us! Lead us into your goodness, into your holiness, into your truth, and into your love with greater faithfulness and courage!'

Friends, what if *now* was the time to hit reset? "Pray that God uses these days as a merciful reset of our lives."

YOU + NEED = COMPASSION

I have a theory: When you think you're better than other people, you tend to look down on other people. But here's the flip side. Your compassion towards others increases when you take seriously the extent of your own need.

As humans, we don't tend to want to acknowledge our own flaws. And don't get me wrong, I'm not saying we should constantly beat ourselves up. But when we simply and honestly accept the fact that we are broken, and that we defy God's commands each and every day, and that each of us is painstakingly lost without the saving mercy of Jesus, we are less harsh towards others—and more compassionate.

Let me quote one of the world's most famous verses about sin, Romans 3:23: "all have sinned and fall short of the glory of God..." Every single person you will meet today has sinned and fallen short of God's glory. But so have you. The good news is that we have been given peace with God—both in this life and the next—not because of how morally good we are, but because of what Jesus has done for us on the cross.

Yup. We are a people of *need*. We *need* God's compassion. We *need* forgiveness. We *need* saving. We *need* help. We *need* strength. We *need* wisdom. And I think that should motivate us to show compassion to the people who need it—just like us.

When you think you're better than other people, you tend to look down on other people. But your compassion towards others increases when you take seriously the extent of your own need.

COMING TO HIM WITH THE GREATEST FREEDOM

Psalm 91:3-4 says, "Surely [God] will save you from the fowler's snare and from the deadly pestilence. He will cover you with his feathers, and under his wings you will find refuge; his faithfulness will be your shield and rampart." (A rampart is a protecting wall.) Save you. Cover you. Refuge. Shield. Rampart. These words speak of the intense care that God has for us personally in times of trial and tribulation.

Reflecting on these verses, the great thinker John Calvin said this: "Since [God] condescends in such a gracious manner to our weakness, surely there is nothing to prevent us from coming to him with the greatest freedom."[22] When Calvin uses the word "condescends," he's not using it in the negative sense we often use it today. What he means is that God lovingly comes to our level and meets us there in order to help us. And that should (a) convince us of the personal and attentive care God has for us, and (b) compel us to bring our concerns to God with greater eagerness and freedom.

Because of this, here's a question I think you need to ask: *What personal and private thoughts and challenges do you need to talk to God about?* Sure, it's good to talk to God in general terms asking for help and strength. But I think you need to talk to God with greater eagerness and freedom about your personal and private thoughts and challenges as well. Ask God to be powerfully present, even if you think the things in your personal and private thoughts are small. After all, what we think is small is sometimes big.

Save you. Cover you. Refuge. Shield. Rampart. These words speak of the intense care that God has for us personally in times of trial and tribulation. What personal and private thoughts and challenges do you need to talk to God about?

FEAR CAN'T RULE OVER YOU IF

What makes some people afraid, and others unafraid? Imagine two men with a similar past, personality and personal life. When hardship comes, the first one loses sleep, perspective and peace. But the other usually sleeps well, maintains perspective, and feels at peace—even though life is sometimes a struggle. The first doesn't trust that God is in control and cares for him. The second does.

Psalm 91:5-6 says, "You will not fear the terror of night, nor the arrow that flies by day, nor the pestilence that stalks in the darkness, nor the plague that destroys at midday." There are terrors in the night, arrows in the day, pestilence that stalks in the darkness, and a plague that destroys at midday. Woah. But at the start of verse 5 it says that you will "not fear" them. Why? Because the Lord "is my refuge and my fortress, my God, in whom I trust" (verse 2).

Here's a question for you to think about: *How does God's care for you make you less fearful?* How would you answer, honestly? Think through some reasons. Name some examples. And grow your confidence that is who he says he is and does what he promises he will do for those who love him.

Fear can't rule over you if God already has the job.

SEEING STRAIGHT IN A TIME OF NAME-CALLING, CONTROVERSY AND SPIN

You don't have to look too far to find controversy. Riots make the news, big internet companies are accused of suppressing speech, 'identity politics' is all over the place, environmental laws seem to get sidelined for economic gain, and there are random shootings in public places. Part of the problem with these hot-button issues is all the rhetoric and spin. Plus, the internet has given people louder voices and bigger platforms to convince you that their ideas are the best ideas.

So in light of extremism, information overload, rhetoric and spin, how do we know the truth and act in a Christ-centred way?

First, know that truth is defined by Jesus. Jesus comes full of "grace and *truth*," is "the way and the *truth* and the life," and if you follow his teachings you will "know the *truth*, and the *truth* will set you free" (John 1:14; 14:6; 8:32, emphasis added). So in and through it all we ask ourselves: What does Jesus or the Bible teach about this?

Second, we act in a loving way because Jesus compels us to love. He says we are to "*love* one another" (John 13:34), and to "*love* your neighbor as yourself" (John 13:34; Matthew 22:39, emphasis added). So in and through it all we also ask ourselves: How can I be more loving toward others in the midst of this?

At the top of the steep and bumpy driveway at our family homestead, there is a huge railway spike in a rock. In the old days, a team of horses would pull up a threshing machine at harvest time. But the driveway was so steep and bumpy that the horses and wagon could stall, go into the ditch, or crash. So close to the top, the wagon was tied off to the railway spike. It was a way to make sure the horses and wagon were permanently secure when things got dicey.

In a time of extremism, information overload, rhetoric and spin, that's what the truth and love of Christ are to you and me: Our railway spike. They keep us permanently secure and on the right path when things get dicey.

FOR THOSE WHO ARE SUFFERING

There is a lot of suffering in the world. There is personal anguish and anxiety. There is the coronavirus and its effects.

There is family and relationship stress. There is discrimination and oppression and violence and war. None of this surprises me because we live in a broken world. But it bothers me. It bothers me because *it's not what God intended.*

So, in a sense, the suffering that is in our lives and world reminds me that all suffering is temporary, and that, one day, God will bring to completion his global renovation and make all things beautiful and new. Revelation 21:4 gives us a glimpse: "'He will wipe every tear from their eyes. There will be no more death' or mourning or crying or pain, for the old order of things has passed away."

Hope doesn't completely pull the knife out of your suffering; but it does assure you that one day your wounds and pain will be a distant memory. The hope of Christ slides in close, puts its arm around you and says, quietly and confidently, 'With me, your greatest joy and peace are not in your past—but still to come.'

Whatever you're going through, have hope. Suffering bothers us because we know it's not supposed to be that way—and one day, it won't be.

THE MORE PROSPEROUS AND EDUCATED WE ARE

When you read through the New Testament healing stories, you start to see some patterns. One is that the people who come to Jesus for help are desperate. Another is that they are convinced he can actually do something about their situation.

For example, in Matthew 9:18 a respectable synagogue leader kneels before Jesus in a posture of humility after his daughter has died and says, "come and put your hand on her, and she will live." Two verses later a woman who has been bleeding for twelve years says, "If I only touch his cloak, I will be healed." Both are desperate, and both are convinced he can actually do something to help.

Let's be honest. Here in North America, a lot of us are doing okay. Even if we're going through some troubles—and if you're reading this in 2020 there have definitely been some troubles!—most of us have a friend to lean on, a hospital to go to, some food in the fridge, medicine to access, some education in the pocket, and some programs to tap. Plus, because we've been saturated by the prevailing cynicism of our society, I wonder how many of us are really convinced that Jesus can do something significant to help our problems.

Roger Olson is a Professor of Ethics. He says, "The more prosperous and educated we are, the more likely we are to substitute our own cleverness and accomplishments for the power of prayer. That's the seductive power of prosperity—it makes us less reliant on God. We think we've got everything under control."[23] And guess what? Here in North America we're generally very prosperous and well-educated!

But no matter who you are, and no matter how "well" you may (or may not) be doing, remember this: We have a loving God who cares *and is able to help*. Despite the illusion of own our "cleverness and accomplishments," the extent to which we need God never dips below one hundred percent.

GOD SOMETIMES USES MIRACLES, BUT HE OFTEN USES THIS

Have you ever prayed for a miracle and it didn't happen? Have you ever wondered why God didn't act? Have you ever been told that you just didn't believe enough? In these moments we can feel very alone or angry or disillusioned—as if God's apparent silence meant (or means) that he doesn't care—or maybe isn't even real.

But consider this. Proverbs 17:17 says, "A friend loves at all times, and a brother is born for a time of adversity." And Ecclesiastes 4:9-10 says, "Two are better than one, because they have a good return for their labor: If either of them falls down, one can help the other up." Do you want to know what these passages make me think? They make me think that God often uses people instead of miracles.

God's power and presence isn't limited to high-drama interventions. In fact, I think he works even more frequently in low-drama interventions. Sure, there are highly dramatic and miraculous events sometimes, but that doesn't mean God is silent or absent when life seems ordinary. It simply means simply that God also works through plain old day-to-day life.

Are you looking for help? Do you need a friend? Do you need to be a friend to somebody else? God often uses people instead of miracles.

WHAT IF GOD WAS EINSTEIN AND WE WERE ANTS?

Imagine that a small child wandered into an operating room at a hospital only to discover their daddy cut open on a table, surrounded by doctors holding knives and wearing weird masks. Oh, and there's blood all over the place. Naturally, the child would scream out, "Nooo! Stop hurting daddy!" The child simply didn't realize that the doctors were performing a triple-bypass surgery. They were doing it to *help* daddy, not hurt him. I've heard it said before that, comparatively speaking, we humans are like ants and God is like Einstein. How could an ant ever really understand what is going on in Einstein's brain?

I share this today because we can sometimes assume that if we don't know the reason for something going on in our lives, that there simply can't be one. But that's like an ant thinking Einstein doesn't know what he's doing simply because the ant doesn't comprehend advanced physics.

In Romans 11:33 Paul writes: "Oh, the depth of the riches of the wisdom and knowledge of God! How unsearchable his judgments, and his paths beyond tracing out!" Evelyn Underhill has said: "If God were small enough to be understood, he wouldn't be big enough to be worshiped."[24]

Do we know some things about God, things that we discover in the Bible? Absolutely! But we don't know everything. His paths are "beyond tracing out." Know this: Through the ups and downs of life, God is still God, and God is still good. And because of that enormous, beautiful gift, we worship him.

"ORDINARY" MIRACLES

It's probably clear that I believe in miracles. In Matthew 19:26 Jesus says, "with God all things are possible." And I fully affirm that God can and does do mind-bending things.

But God doesn't just work in dramatic ways—he works in "ordinary" ways too. The reason I put "ordinary" in quotes is because what we often think is normal and coincidental is actually providential. Let's say, for example, that you've been praying for a miracle. Let's also say that because you can't see anything happening immediately that you assume God has decided to take a pass on getting personally involved in this particular problem. But it was God who created natural laws and biological processes. Therefore, God can also work his healing power through what we might consider "ordinary" people and events: medical appointments, physiotherapy, psychotherapy, and Tylenol!

When God doesn't dramatically intervene in a way we can

see, we can mistakenly believe the Devil's lies that come quickly and quietly to our ears: "God doesn't care... He's not there... Why bother with him if he doesn't bother with you?" The Devil loves to use your trails to turn you against God. But don't believe him, and don't let him.

Jesus said that "with God all things are possible." I don't think he was just referring to high-drama interventions, but low-drama interventions too. What we often think is normal and coincidental is actually providential.

WHEN BAD THINGS AMPLIFY GOOD THINGS

Recently I threw out my back. Again. It frustrated me. I'm a super-motivated person who likes to be doing things. And there I was, relegated to my bed for large swaths of my day. I could hear my watch ticking—as if it was taunting me! You're right. I probably need to relax more. But do you want to know what the whole thing caused me to do more? Pray. In this sense, something good came out of something bad. I'm not saying that all bad things are good things. But *bad things can be used to amplify good things.*

In Philippians 4:12 Paul writes, "I have learned the secret of being content in any and every situation, whether well fed or hungry, whether living in plenty or in want." And what is that secret? That as he goes about serving God: "I can do all this through him who gives me strength."

So what is happening in your life right now that is bad? Maybe it's some kind of less-than-ideal situation that makes you want to kick the wall in frustration or run for the hills. But lean on Christ and make the best of it. Look for how it can draw you closer—instead of push you further—from God. I'm not saying that all bad things are good things. But bad things can be used to amplify good things.

ACCESS TO THE GREATEST POWER ON EARTH

Listen to Paul's powerful prayer in Ephesians 3:16-17: "I pray that out of [God's] glorious riches he may strengthen you with power through his Spirit in your inner being, so that Christ may dwell in your hearts through faith."

When you decide to be a Christian — that is, when you acknowledge your brokenness and sin before God, ask for his forgiveness, trust what Jesus did for you on the cross, and make him the Lord and boss of your life — God himself in the person of the Holy Spirit begins to dwell and live inside of you in a new way. I think we can sometimes neglect or undervalue that life-changing fact!

If you played hockey and your team had the chance to enlist Wayne Gretzky in his prime, would you do it? If you could go back in time and hear a speech and have a personal conversation with Martin Luther King Jr, would you do it? Of course! If you had access to the greatest power on earth, don't you think you'd jump at the opportunity? If you're a Christian, you do, and you can.

May prayer for you is Paul's prayer to the Ephesians: "I pray that out of God's glorious riches he may strengthen you with power through his Spirit in your inner being, so that Christ may dwell in your hearts through faith. Ask the Holy Spirit to use you in powerful ways, and be open to his guidance.

HE WANTS YOUR WHOLE HEART—AND YOUR HEART WHOLE

Your mental health and well-being is critically important to your overall well-being.

It matters to you, the people around you, and God. Max Lucado says that God "wants not only your whole heart; he wants your heart whole."[25]

But mental health doesn't get talked about very much. There's a lot of misunderstanding. Maybe it's because some people think that wounds you *can* see are more important than wounds you *can't* see. But just because it's hard to see something that doesn't mean we should close our eyes.

The reason I bring this up is because *intentionally cultivating gratitude can actually benefit your mental health*. Studies say that gratitude improves psychological health, enhances empathy and reduces aggression, and improves self-esteem. From a faith perspective, *gratitude grounds you in the good God has done, is doing and will do*. When you deliberately reflect on the good that God has done in your past, you're reminded of the good God is doing in your present, and also the good he will do in your future too. He is consistent: the same yesterday, today and forever. Therefore, his presence and guidance endures through all your ups and downs. Psalm 136 recounts all the ways God has been faithful to his people. And after every line it says: "His love endures forever." Not "endured" (past tense), but endures (continuous).

Cultivating intentional gratitude won't make all of your troubles go away. But it is a piece of the puzzle that will improve your mental well-being. Gratitude grounds you in the good God has done, is doing, and will do. God wants not only your whole heart; he wants your heart whole.

FOR A HEALTHIER AND BETTER-GROUNDED YOU

According to the *Canadian Association of Mental Health*, mental illness affects people of all ages and backgrounds. Suicide accounts for twenty-four percent of all deaths for 15-24 year olds. And by age forty, about fifty percent of people in my country will have or have had a mental illness. That's why it's important to be proactive about our mental well-being and to be open about it.

One of the things that we can do to help with that is to worship God intentionally and regularly. Some of you already do that. Some of you never do that. Some of you do it occasionally. Some of you don't know if it makes a difference or what it has to do with mental health.

So let me give your brain something to chew on. Worship draws our eyes back to the awesome permanence and goodness of God. Maybe that's why a 2017 study out of Vanderbilt University says that non-worshipers have higher levels of stress and more risks to their health.[26]

Psalm 96:9 says: "Worship the LORD in the splendor of his holiness..." That reminds us that worship is about fixing our gaze on God; it's about him (not just us); it's about how great God is (not about how good we are); and worship reminds us about the God who never leaves or fails us, even through the jilting ups and downs of life. It's harder to get pulled down by negative things if your mind is more frequently focused on the one big awesome thing.

As I write this, the church I pastor isn't meeting in the building on Sundays for worship. We're in the middle of the COVID-19 pandemic. And, to be honest, I'm not sure how long we'll be in this situation. But one thing is clear: God's people can worship him wherever they are, pandemic or not!

Worship isn't a one-stop cure-all for all your woes. But it's an important piece of the puzzle—which, when assembled, shows a healthier and better grounded you. Worship intentionally and regularly.

DAILY UNEXPECTED PROVIDENCE

In his book *Miracles*, Lee Strobel tells a story about Roger Olson. He was very distraught after a bad medical appointment. The next day an old hymn about God's comfort kept going through Roger's head. Over and over.

On the following Sunday, the pastor in church announced that they would all sing hymn number 220 together: 'Crown Him With Many Crowns.' But when Roger opened the hymnal to number 220 it wasn't 'Crown Him With Many Crowns'; it was the hymn of comfort that had been coursing through his brain all week! But why was everyone singing 'Crown Him' if the pastor had announced the wrong number?

Well, as it turns out, he hadn't. The hymnal Roger picked up wasn't supposed to be there. In fact, it didn't match any of the other hymnals in the pews! This random hymnal, totally out of place, just so happened to include number 220 as the hymn of comfort that had been powerfully repeating in his head all week after his bad appointment. Sure, it could have been a coincidence. But it could also have been God's way of saying to Roger, 'Even though your medical appointment didn't turn out like you wanted, I'm still with you. Roger, it will be okay.'[27]

Speaking about Jesus' supremacy in Colossians 1:17, Paul writes: "in him all things hold together." It's a comment about God's providence. That in him, God sustains all things and guides his people. I think that includes the ways he sustains, guides and comforts us through conversations, circumstances, and eyebrow-raising moments like the "wrong" hymn in a hymnal.

In Jesus "all things hold together." So pay attention. Keep your brain open. He is sustaining, guiding and comforting you through all the ups and downs of life.

THE ONE LABEL THAT MATTERS MOST

Labels. We put them on clothing. But we also put them on people. Sometimes they're labels other people put on us. Labels like "friend" or "classmate" or "co-worker." But there are also labels like "jerk" or "ugly" or "enemy."

And do you know what? We put labels on ourselves as well. Some are good. But some are bad. For some strange, twisted reason, we sometimes believe the worst about ourselves because we know our own failings the best. That's why we need to continually remind ourselves about the victorious label that matters most, and which reminds all the other labels to get in the back seat.

For those of us who follow Christ, our primary label and identity is in Christ. We are *Christ*-ians. Listen to what Paul says in Galatians 2:20: "I have been crucified with Christ and I no longer live, but Christ lives in me. The life I now live in the body, I live by faith in the Son of God, who loved me and gave himself for me." Bam!

That's the label and identity that matters most. Christian. It means "of Christ." It's closely related to "child of God," "disciple," and "son/daughter of the King." That's what ultimately defines you. Nothing else.

I have a way of reminding myself about this wonderful fact. Sometimes at home, when I need the reminder, I find a tap, turn on the water, and splash myself in the face three times while saying, "I am baptized in the name of the Father, and of the Son, and of the Holy Spirit." Maybe that sounds weird. But I'm okay with weird. And no, I'm not re-baptizing myself! I'm simply reminding myself about *who* I am and *whose* I am.

If you're a baptized follower of Jesus, why not do the same? In this negative and crazy world, we all need the reminder. "I no longer live, but Christ lives in me."

We are defined by Christ—not the labels others put on you, and not even the labels you put on yourself. We are his. And there's nothing that anyone can say or do that can alter that life-giving and liberating fact.

MAKE TIME FOR FUN

Having fun is fun. But do you know what? Some people probably don't do fun things as much as they should. Or, when they do something fun, they feel bad about it. Why? Because they know about people who are struggling, and feel bad or guilty that they're out having a good time anyway.

But today I'd like to encourage you to *make time to do fun things*. Granted, I don't think it's wise if your idea of "fun" is knocking mailboxes off their poles with a bat, painting graffiti, or getting blitzed out of your mind. What I'm talking about here is God-honouring fun that puts a smile on your face and renews your soul.

If you're reading this in the COVID-19 pandemic, and if physical distancing rules are still in effect, you might need to get creative. After all, going on an outing with some friends, or watching a sporting event or concert might not be possible. But there are still things you can do to renew yourself for the battle of life. I know someone who organized an online talent show. Someone else made an effort to trek a new hiking trail. Another person has re-discovered old board games and videos games from their youth.

Ecclesiastes 3:1 and 4 says: "There is a time for everything, and a season for every activity under the heavens... a time to weep and a time to laugh..." Wouldn't your days be more renewing if, alongside cultivating your relationship with God, you intentionally made time for some laughter? Life can get tough. So make time for fun.

STAYING OUT OF A HOLE

Structures give us stability when we're wobbly or feeling uncertain. Think of a railing beside a set of stairs.

In a similar way, you can put your schedule together in a specific, helpful way. You can *structure* your week to be continually reminded of God's goodness. Scheduled prayer and Bible reading are a part of godly *structure*. Worship services are a part of godly *structure*. Outings with soul-lifting friends are a part of godly *structure*. Appointed times for rest is a part of godly *structure*. Consistent exercise is a part of godly *structure*.

Isaiah 26:3 (ESV) says, "You keep him in perfect peace whose mind is stayed on you, because he trusts in you." I love the use of the word *stayed* in this context. It carries the implication of being rooted, secure, fixed. Working godly structure into your life *stays* you on God.

Having been through a few bunkers myself I can tell you this: *It's easier to stay out of a hole than climb out of a hole.* So friends, especially those of you who are struggling right now, intentionally structure your week to be continually reminded of God's goodness. *Structure* for success.

YOUR RELIABILITY CAN MAKE AN IMPACT

Being a person of your word helps the people around you. In fact, when you are steady for other people when they're going through a tough time, that stabilizing impact can last for generations.

Not many people know Don Sutton. But he was a pro baseball player for twenty-one seasons. He wasn't flashy. But in 1986 he became one of only thirteen pitchers to win 300 games. "I never considered myself flamboyant or exceptional," he said. "But all my life I've found a way to get the job done."[28] As a result he's been called the "family sedan" of baseball pitchers. Others would come and go. But Sutton persisted.

That could be you. You may not be flashy. But if you are a person who is counted as trustworthy, as someone who consistently keeps their word to other people, you can be that steadfast person in someone else's life when times get tough. *Your reliability is someone else's stability.*

In Galatians 6:9 Paul writes, "Let us not become weary in doing good…" Don't be weary. Instead, be reliable and steadfast in the good you bring into other people's lives—consistently. You don't have to be an All Star. But you can be consistent. Your reliability is someone else's stability.

GOODER

None of us can deny that friendships have a huge impact on us. Ecclesiastes 4:9-10 says, "Two are better than one, because they have a good return for their labor: If either of them falls down, one can help the other up."

How many of us can think of a time when a good friend helped us through something tough? When we think about our friendships, it's easy to think about what we *get* out of the relationship. We wonder, 'Does so-and-so support *me*? Do they help *me*? Are they there for *me*?' There's nothing wrong with that. It's just not the whole picture.

I have a saying. It's that *good friends make good friends gooder*. I realize "gooder" isn't a word. But it seems more memorable when I say it like that! So just as your good friends can support and strengthen you—and make you "gooder"—you should also be a person who supports and strengthens *them*. When they ask themselves that same set of questions—questions like whether or not you support *them* and help *them* and are there for *them*—would they answer Yes?

I realize that none of us have a perfect track record. But when it comes to cultivating quality friendships, we should be equally as concerned with what we *give* as with what we *get*.

"If either of them falls down, one can help the other up." Sometimes you're the one who does the falling. But sometimes you're the one who does the helping. Good friends make good friends gooder.

WHAT HE DID WITH HIS HARDSHIP

When we hear about other people going through hardship in a noble way, it can actually be a source of encouragement for us. First, we sympathize with their situation and offer help. But it can also make us think: 'If they can do it, so can I!' We can learn from their example.

Recently I was at the church of Hyeon Soo Lim. He is the pastor who was imprisoned in North Korea for his faith. Fortunately he was released last year. Praise God! For two years he was forced to do hard labour. He had to dig holes in the frozen ground with his bare hands. He also had to break apart chunks of coal. Upon his return he talked about his battle with terrible loneliness. So, what did he do? Mope around in an endless pity-party? He spent what little free time he had by reading one hundred books on North Korea, reading the Bible in English and Korean five times, memorizing more than seven hundred Bible verses, and worshiping alone for one hundred and thirty Sundays. Hardship can draw you closer—or push you further—from God. Hyeon Soo Lim chose to draw closer. What an example!

In Romans 8:39 Paul says that nothing "will be able to separate us from the love of God that is in Christ Jesus our Lord." That includes imprisonment, hard labour and loneliness—and it also includes bad days, feeling sad, regret and stress. The reason I say this is because I know that many of you are going through a tough time right now. So believe what the Bible says in Romans 8:39, and be encouraged and inspired by the example of Hyeon Soo Lim. Hardship can draw you closer —or push you further—from God. Which do you choose?

THE HELPEE

I want to talk with you about love—but from an angle you maybe haven't thought much about. Usually when we think about love, we think about how God wants us to be proactive in the love we have for one another. In John 13:34 Jesus says, "As I have loved you, so you must love one another." And then in Matthew 22:39 he says to "love your neighbor as yourself." Being proactive about love is something to strive for.

But how many of you are good at *accepting* help from someone else? After all, if you're supposed to be loving toward one another, that means that sometimes you'll be the one giving it, but sometimes you'll be the one *receiving* it. The reason it's important to think this through is because a lot of us are not very good at accepting help from others. And yet, the help people offer us is often an expression of their love for us.

Many of us want to be "strong and independent." And that can be good in many situations—very good. But with that mindset we can also dismiss the help people offer us because we think it means we can't handle stuff on our own. But that doesn't make you strong. It makes you stubborn.

Sometimes you're the helper. And sometimes you're the helpee. And that's okay. All of us need God. And more often than not, we need one another too.

WALK TALL

In 2013, a book came out by Robert Galbraith called *The Cuckoo's Calling*. It was a crime fiction novel. The reviews were fantastic, but it didn't sell very well—just 1500 print copies and a few thousand online. But the Sunday Times learned that "Robert Galbraith" was a pseudonym—a pen name. The real author was none other than J.K. Rowling, the popular author of the Harry Potter series! As soon as that information was released to the public, sales jumped by 156,866%! It zoomed to number 1. The difference was a name, the record and reputation of the one holding the pen.[29]

In Acts 11:26 we read, "The disciples were called Christians first at Antioch." Jesus' followers were given a name: *Christ*-ian. It means "of Christ." And as we know, names can, in some situations, carry a powerful weight. Well, Christ has "the name that is above every name" (Philippians 2:9). And if you've pledged your allegiance to Christ, it's a name you can claim as your own—a name that has infinite value, dignity, worth and purpose. You are "of Christ, and Christ is of God" (1 Corinthians 3:23). Because of that, no one can diminish your worth; no one can degrade your dignity; and no one can thwart your purpose. Today, whatever you're facing, walk tall.

THE GOOD NEWS ABOUT YOUR WEAKNESS

One of the mistakes we often make is to pretend we have it all together when we don't.

It happens innocently enough. A lot of us are doing our prayerful best to grow and become more like Jesus. But we can exaggerate or embellish our progress!

Take me for example. I often don't have answers to all the questions. I sometimes feel tired and sad. I can resent all the hard work. Thoughts creep into my mind that I know shouldn't be there. I can get apathetic about the plight of others. I sometimes do the easy thing instead of the right thing. Friends, I'm a *bona fide* sinner. And I mean it.

But get this. In 2 Corinthians 12:7-8 Paul describes a "thorn" in his flesh. He's fuzzy on details, but it's clearly a weakness, a hindrance. (By the way, I've done the math and by my count I'm pretty sure I have four such thorns!) But Paul is told that God's "power is made perfect in weakness" (verse 9). That changes his perspective. That's why he goes on to say, "For when I am weak, then I am strong" (verse 10). When we acknowledge our weakness, we're more honest and allow God's power to work through us all the more!

If we think it's all up to us, and that our own personal strength is the only thing that counts, we close ourselves to the power of Christ working in and through us. Why wouldn't we want that? He's the greatest source of power in the universe!

Self-reliance is God-resistance. So let's stop faking perfection, be more honest, and let God work in and through us. "For when I am weak, then I am strong."

THE BEST IS YET TO COME

People have a tonne of misconceptions about heaven. One is that it's going to be boring. This sentiment is captured in a *Far Side* comic where some dude sits on a cloud, bored out of his skull, saying "wish I'd brought a magazine." But in Philippians 1:23, the apostle Paul says: "My desire is to depart and be with Christ, for that is far better" (ESV). The key word is *better*. He still has important work to do in this world and in this life, but if he were to die and go to Christ he knows it would be *better*.

Think of some of your best experiences in life. A wonderful family memory? Disney world? A tremendous achievement? Reuniting with a long-lost friend? Climbing Everest? Bringing a new life into the world? A meaningful mission trip? Heaven is *better* than every single one of those experiences! If you're not hungry for heaven, you've been misinformed.

Steven Curtis Chapman is a well-known Christian singer. In May 2008 he and his wife, Mary Beth, were devastated when their 5-year old daughter, Maria, was killed in a car accident. Many people sent in words of comfort and support. But one conversation stood out that really helped him. It was with pastor Greg Laurie who could relate to their experience because he had also lost a child in a car accident. Thinking ahead to heaven, and knowing how amazing it would be, here is what he said to Chapman: "Remember, your future with Maria is infinitely greater than your past with her."[30]

Hope is the wind that lifts your soul through the darkest days. So, no matter what you're going through, cling to Christ and have hope. The best is yet to come.

EVERYTHING GOOD IN LIFE MULTIPLIED TIMES GOD

Heaven. It will be anything but boring. It will be far better than anything we can experience on this earth. That can give us great hope through whatever we're dealing with because the best is always yet to come.

Here's something else about heaven. Psalm 16:11 (ESV) says that in God's presence "there is fullness of joy." So we know it will be a place of joy. And not partial-ness of joy, but *full*-ness of joy! No more tears, cancer, or car accidents. No more financial worries, disappointments, or friends ignoring you. No more family feuds, painful relationships, or frustrating work. No more social injustice, pollution, or cynicism. No more anxiety, despair, or sleepless nights. No more panic attacks, joint pain, or sick children. Hospitals won't even exist!

No more. Las Vegas Pastor Jud Wilhite says that heaven like "will be everything good in life, multiplied times God, minus all the pain, sorrow, fear, injustice, and loss."[31]

Today, take a moment to think about heaven, and let a smile slide across your face. Thinking about it won't make all of your challenges go away, but it can lift your spirits to know that hope is always on the horizon. *Hardship is temporary, but joy is for eternity.*

EVEN WHEN WE DON'T UNDERSTAND

Marshall Shelley tells the story of the birth of his son. When the child was in the womb, he and his wife Susan learned that he had an abnormal heart. This was obviously difficult for them. They were told their baby would probably not survive birth. The child might not even make it to full term. So they prayed. They prayed for a miracle! When the time for delivery came, the child was born, alive. They were so happy. Marshall writes, "He was a healthy pink, and we saw his chest rise and fall. The breath of life. Thank you, God."

But two minutes later, the child stopped breathing. He died. Joy was followed by misery. The nurse asked if they had a name for the baby. And the mother said, "Toby." She offered an explanation: "It's short for a biblical name, Tobiah, which means 'God is good.'"[32]

I think of Psalm 31:19: "How abundant are the good things that you have stored up for those who fear you, that you bestow in the sight of all, on those who take refuge in you." The Shelleys believed that God is good when everything is good and makes sense, and even when everything is not good and when it doesn't make sense.

Life can be very difficult. I'm not diminishing that. But even then, we can trust that God is still good, loving, righteous and holy—when we understand it, and even when we don't. As we read in Psalm 46:1-2: "God is our refuge and strength, an ever-present help in trouble. Therefore we will not fear…" Trust in the Lord. He is your strength and hope. "How abundant are the good things that you have stored up for those who fear you, that you bestow in the sight of all, on those who take refuge in you."

DEALING WITH STRESS

Have you ever dealt with stress? Wow, all of your hands just shot up at once. Dr. Tim Cantopher explains that the word "stress" is from the world of engineering. Think of a bridge. When it is bearing a load that is heavier than it is designed to carry, it is "under stress." With that in mind, here is how he defines stress: "Stress is experienced when a person is pulled or pushed in a direction that they would not normally take, or at a pace at which they would not normally proceed, or with an impetus that they would not normally experience. They are enduring a force for which they are not designed."[33] Yup. So what's to be done?

Quietness. Psalm 46:10 famously says, "Be still, and know that I am God..." Lamentations 3:26 also comes to mind: "it is good to wait quietly for the salvation of the Lord." It can be hard to hear God's voice of grace when you're running at a breakneck pace. Quietness. It doesn't make all your stress go away, but it can slowly re-introduce a more peaceful perspective when your brain is full of frantic voices and pressures you were not designed to bear.

Go for a walk. Shut off your phone. Go for a drive in the country. Saunter. Carve out some alone time. Close your eyes to pray... and just listen. Cultivate quietness. Listen for the Lord. And rise above a load you were never designed to bear.

THE BIG PICTURE

There's something that people I admire have in common. They have the ability to see the big picture even when times are hard, and even when they're under pressure. As a result, they don't get thrown off course. They're more likely to hold to their principles. And they're less likely to say or do something that they'll regret later.

Paul's words in Colossians 3:1-3 are classic big picture thinking: "Since, then, you have been raised with Christ, set your hearts on things above, where Christ is, seated at the right hand of God. Set your minds on things above, not on earthly things. For you died, and your life is now hidden with Christ in God." That's big stuff. One of the things Paul is saying to the Colossians—and to us—is that since they have already received the benefits of being "raised with Christ" (even though they're still physically living life on earth), they can focus on "things above" and not get distracted and pulled down by what belongs to their "earthly nature." (He gives some examples in verses 5, 8 and 9).

Focusing on the big picture is trusting in God's plan—even when you not sure what tomorrow will bring. It's letting "the peace of Christ rule in your hearts" (verse 15)—even when you're tempted to let worry and fear take over. It's marching forward in God's mission with humility and love as your close companions—even when you want to yell at everyone and run for the hills. And it's about prayer.

In a book about preaching, teacher and pastor David Helm offers some helpful advice for fellow preachers, which just so happens to be wise counsel for everyone else too: "The more you spend time looking at the big picture, the better your grasp of the big picture will be."[34] It's challenging, especially when our lives and world feel pretty messed up. But a grasp of the big picture will help you avoid getting stuck in the weeds of doubt, worry, fear, anger and panic.

Set your hearts on things above. "The more you spend time looking at the big picture, the better your grasp of the big picture will be."

CAN YOU IMAGINE THE SUN WITH NO HEAT?

The apostle John had a very simple and direct way of saying things: "Whoever does not love does not know God, because God is love" (1 John 4:8). He's saying that if you don't love, then you don't know God. Love is so central to who God is, that we can't neglect it in our own lives.

Commenting on these very verses in the 16th century, the great Reformer John Calvin wrote: "For when any one separates faith from love, it is the same as though he attempted to take away heat from sun."[35] Can you imagine the sun without heat? Neither can I. That's like faith without love. This doesn't mean we don't have bad days, or that we never sin. What it *does* mean is that, if we truly know God in Christ, we will know the importance of love and will be moving in that direction.

"For when any one separates faith from love, it is the same as though he attempted to take away heat from sun."[36]

YOUR VICTORY IN LIFE

A lot of people struggle with an identity of failure. Their sense of self is saturated with thoughts, ideas and voices like, "I'm not good enough," "I'm not smart enough," "I'm not pretty enough," or "I'm not successful enough." But the resurrection changes that. When we more fully understand the significance of Jesus' resurrection, we realize that *his* victory over death is *our* victory in life. *His* triumph is *our* triumph; *his* hope is *our* hope; and *his* joy is *our* joy. What happened to Jesus is a kind of foreshadowing of what will one day happen to everyone who follows him.

Death will whimper. We will be given spiritual, resurrected bodies. Decay and pain will go six feet under. All things will be made new. And God's justice, truth and healing love with reign supreme. In the meantime, you can know that "your labor in the Lord is not in vain" (verse 58). God can use every prayer, every act of faith, mercy and care, and every word of truth and encouragement, for his kingdom-building purposes in the world.

So whenever those voices of failure start to buzz around your brain, blow them up with these words from 1 Corinthians 15:57: "thanks be to God! He gives us the victory through our

Lord Jesus Christ." No matter what you're going through, move you from an identity of failure to an identity of victory. Jesus' victory over death is your victory in life.

JOY REIGNED SUPREME

It's significant that Christians worship on Sundays. It was—and is—the day of the resurrection of Jesus. No matter what time of year it is, and no matter how old you are, and no matter what you're doing through, it's a reminder of the resurrection and how central it is to our faith.

Viktor Frankl was a holocaust survivor. Here's how he described learning about the end of the war: "...the camp gate was thrown open. A splendid, aluminum-colored car, on which were painted large red crosses, slowly rolled on to the parade ground... Who worried about [the need to] escape now? Boxes with medicines were unloaded from the car, cigarettes were distributed, we were photographed and joy reigned supreme."[37]

"Joy reigned supreme." I love that. Joy is bigger than happiness. It doesn't always have a smile; but it has victory and hope carved on the heart. Quoting the prophet Isaiah, Paul talks about the resurrection like this: "Death has been swallowed up in victory" (1 Corinthians 15:54). In Jesus, we have something that cannot be intimidated—not even by death!

You don't always feel like smiling. I get that. But joy is bigger than happiness. It has victory and hope carved on the heart. You remember that the resurrection happened. But don't forget what happened at the resurrection. Joy reigned supreme. And it still can.

THE ONLY COMFORT IN LIFE AND DEATH

Some of you are baptized, perhaps many of you. That's so wonderful. So let me offer a few thoughts about it.

First, the waters of baptism are not magic juice that get you into heaven. That's an important point. If someone has come to believe in Christ and then happens to die suddenly before they are baptized, God isn't going to reject them on a technicality. Why? Because biblical teachings don't make salvation dependent on baptism.

Second, baptism is what we might call a sign and seal of our new union with Christ. It is a very special moment that symbolizes dying to our old life, being washed and forgiven of sin, and being raised up through the waters into our new life in Christ. We emerge with a new allegiance, loyalty, and purpose in life. Think of a wedding ceremony. I've led many of them. When the couple gets married, they make a commitment to one other, and then they exchange rings. The ring doesn't make you married; and if you take it off you're not all of a sudden not married. It is a reminder of the union. Just like baptism.

In a profound document from the sixteen century called the *Heidelberg Catechism* we read this: "Question: What is your only comfort in life and death? Answer: That I am not my own, but belong with body and soul, both in life and in death, to my faithful Saviour Jesus Christ." That is the greatest comfort of all. And nothing in this big, troubled world, can ever wrestle it away from you.

ENGAGE IN S.S.T.

Do you ever see things online that really upset you? And have you wanted to go into attack mode, jump down someone's throat, or log on with guns-a-blazin'?

Speaking to the church in Ephesians 4:2-3, Paul writes: "Be completely humble and gentle; be patient, bearing with one another in love. Make every effort to keep the unity of the Spirit through the bond of peace." I'm guessing that's going to be easier to do when we engage in S.S.T. It stands for *Sober Second Thought*. It's easy to skip in an age when we can go online and literally say or comment anything instantly without taking even a few minutes to think about it.

I knew someone who posted something online that they almost instantly regretted. They deleted their post. But it was too late. Someone had already taken a screen shot of what they had posted, saved it, and re-posted their mistake for everyone to see… and criticize… forever.

The internet is a tricky business. And let's be honest: When we're going through challenging times we're not always at our best. So be thoughtful and engage in S.S.T. "Be completely humble and gentle; be patient, bearing with one another in love. Make every effort to keep the unity of the Spirit through the bond of peace."

TIME AND TRUST

"I trust in you, Lord; I say, 'You are my God'" (Psalm 31:14).

By spending time with someone you quite often learn to trust them. Why? Because you start to know what makes them tick. You become more familiar with their words and ways. You appreciate the mutual investment of time—and that can build trust.

So it is with God.

And let me tell you this. Trust matters. We all know it's true. When you're in trouble, who do you talk to? Someone you *trust*. When you're confused, who do you talk to? Someone you *trust*. When you're feeling overwhelmed, who do you talk to? Someone you *trust*.

Brother Lawrence was a French monk from the 17th century. He was known for a humble-but-powerful reliance on God through each and every day of life. He spent time with God, even when he was going about his daily chores. In a short collection of his writings, he offers this penetrating insight: "The world, the flesh, and the devil join forces and assault the soul so straitly and so untiringly that, without humble reliance on the ever-present aid of God, they drag the soul down in spite of all resistance... We must go about our labours quietly, calmly, and lovingly, entreating Him to prosper the works of our hands; by thus keeping heart and mind fixed on God, we shall bruise the head of the evil one, and beat down his weapons to the ground."[38]

That is the perspective of someone who has spent time with God, and who has learned to trust God. So spend time with God. Learn to trust him. And in so doing, you shall bruise the head of the evil one, and beat down his weapons to the ground!

Here are some ideas about how to spend time with God. Talk to him when you go about routine tasks. Admire his creation when you go for a walk. Set aside time to read the Bible. Recite some of his promises when you're in bed or driving in the car.

When times are tough we need people to trust. As Charles Haddon Spurgeon said in the nineteen-century: "God is too good to be unkind and He is too wise to be mistaken. And when we cannot trace His hand, we must trust His heart."[39]

HEARING BACK FROM GOD

Have you ever talked to someone, but they just sit there in silence, never saying anything back? It ends the conversation pretty quickly, doesn't it? Silence tends to make you think that the other person isn't listening, or doesn't care.

That's how a lot of people feel about prayer. Since they tend to do all the talking and can't hear God talking back, they figure God either isn't listening, or doesn't care. But that's not true. Bible verses abound about God listening and responding to prayer. But what I want to highlight today is one of the ways God does in fact talk back to you through prayer.

In a classic book about prayer called *With Christ in the School of Prayer*, Andrew Murray cites an old saying: "I pray—I speak to my Father; I read—my Father speaks to me."[40] Your words often come out of your mouth. God's words often come out of the Bible. As Psalm 119:130 says: "The unfolding of your words gives light; it gives understanding to the simple."

Personally, I usually use the Bible when I pray. I talk to God, then read a Bible passage, then talk to God again, and then read some more. What I often discover is that a one-way monologue turns into two-way conversation. His eternal words start to speak wisdom directly into my day-to-day situations and problems. "I pray—I speak to my Father; I read—my Father speaks to me."

THE DEVIL'S ACHILLES HEEL

Imagine we're playing a football game, but we can't see an opponent. So we obviously think the game is going to be pretty easy. But as it begins we keep running into invisible roadblocks and frustrations. This makes us scratch our heads. Why isn't this easier? But then someone tells us that we've been misinformed: We actually *do* have an opponent, but it's an *invisible* opponent. All of a sudden that changes everything. We learn more about our opponent, take them seriously, and equip ourselves accordingly!

I realize it's not a popular or easy topic, but this is what I think it's like when we pretend the Devil and his minions aren't there. When you read through the Gospels, Jesus and his followers took the invisible-but-real battle between good and evil *very* seriously, and they equipped themselves accordingly. Ephesians 6:12 says: "Our struggle is not against flesh and blood, but against...the powers of this dark world and against the spiritual forces of evil..."

The good news is that there is no need to fear: *The Devil's Achilles' heel is biblical truth and prayer in Jesus' name.* So root yourself in biblical truth, and pray for protection against the evil one who would love nothing better than to intimidate and unplug Jesus' people from being his hands and feet of truth and love in the world.

Do you get frustrated in life because you're living as if there's no one on the other side of the football field? Jesus and his followers took the invisible-but-real battle between good and evil seriously, and they equipped themselves accordingly. So should we. The Devil's Achilles heel is biblical truth and prayer in Jesus' name.

THE EXPANDING EFFECT IN YOUR HEART AND MIND

Viktor Frankl was a neurologist and psychiatrist. He was also a Holocaust survivor who was no stranger to hardship. In his book *Man's Search for Meaning* he says that "it is possible to practice the art of living even in a concentration camp, although suffering is omnipresent." He goes on to offer this analogy:

> *man's suffering is similar to the behavior of gas. If a certain quantity of gas is pumped into an empty chamber, it will fill the chamber completely and evenly, no matter how big the chamber. Thus suffering completely fills the human soul and conscious mind, no matter whether the suffering is great or little. Therefore the "size" of human suffering is absolutely relative.*

It's a profound insight. And I think that many of us know it to be true. Even though we know other people have struggles that are "worse" than ours, since we are the ones who are personally experiencing our own hardship, it has an expanding effect in our hearts and minds because it is still "big" to us. It's like gas that expands to fit every corner of a room.

But Frankl doesn't stop there. "It follows," he writes, "that a very trifling thing can cause the greatest of joys." Just as a hardship can expand and fill the "human soul and conscious mind," so can small things which have the capacity to bring us joy. In the concentration camps, Frankl and the others experienced unimaginable horrors. And yet, at the same time, he was able to reflect on ways he and others experienced happiness. At one point he even made a balance sheet to keep track of them. He remembers being transferred to Dachau which he had heard was less severe than Auschwitz, and a guard who distributed soup evenly and didn't show favourites![41]

In 1 Thessalonians 5 Paul tells his readers to encourage one another as they wait for the return of Jesus. "Rejoice always, pray continually, give thanks in all circumstances; for this is God's will for you in Christ Jesus" (1 Thessalonians 6:16-18). When you're going through a hard time, maybe you just don't feel like it. But what if identifying things to rejoice over, praying continually, and showing gratitude through the ups and downs of life had an expanding effect in your mind? And what if they were able to rival the darkness which is doing its best to dominate the real estate in your soul?

"Rejoice always, pray continually, give thanks in all circumstances; for this is God's will for you in Christ Jesus."

WHY YOUR BROKENNESS CAN BE USEFUL

All of us carry a certain amount of brokenness. These are problems we have, mistakes we've made, good-plans-gone-wrong that weight us down like the proverbial tonne of bricks. Because we think of these things as negative, we think they have no redeeming value.

But know this: *Your temporary brokenness can have eternal usefulness.* Here's what I mean. First, all of your brokenness is *temporary*. On the other side of death, we'll all quickly realize that life on earth was a short sprint, and that who we were then isn't who we'll always be. We will be remade. Second, the experiences you've had—even the negative ones—can have eternal *usefulness*. In other words, because of what you've been through, you can now have a unique perspective, or a more understanding attitude, or some hard-fought wisdom that might benefit someone else who is struggling through something similar. It might just be what someone else needs to get them through, to open up to God, and to muster hope for a new day.

In Romans 8:28 Paul writes, "we know that in all things God works for the good of those who love him, who have been called according to his purpose." This doesn't mean that all things are good, but that, for those who love him and have been called according to God's purpose, that all things can work together for good.

Just because you've had challenging experiences, that

doesn't mean those experiences are wasted. You may now have a unique experience, or a more understanding attitude, or some hard-fought wisdom that can significantly help someone else who's going through a hard time. Your temporary brokenness can have eternal usefulness.

HE SPAT ON ME

I was driving up the four lane highway about to go under a bridge. I noticed a guy just standing there on top of the bridge looking down at the traffic. As I drove under he spat on me! He had great aim because it went right in the middle of my windshield. What do you do in a situation like that? Do you stick your arm out the window and make a gesture that is unbecoming of a minister of the Gospel? Don't worry, I didn't do that! I just used my windshield wipers and kept on truckin'.

It's a simple illustration about life. There are many times when someone else's bad attitude can tarnish yours. They do something to insult, threaten or degrade you, and it tempts you to return the favour. In 1 Peter 3:9 the apostle was counselling Christians in circumstances way more serious than being spat on. They were being severely persecuted for their faith. This is what he said: "Do not repay evil with evil or insult with insult. On the contrary, repay evil with blessing, because to this you were called so that you may inherit a blessing."

In life, people will do things to insult, threaten or degrade you. But think of Christ. Think of his great love for you and for others. Because of that, don't play their game—plays yours. Don't contribute to the mess, just bless. Don't let someone else's attitude tarnish yours.

THE AGE OF MELANCHOLY

Psychologist Daniel Goleman says that we live in the Age of Melancholy. Here is how he describes it:

> Each successive generation worldwide since the opening of the century has lived with a higher risk than their parents of suffering a major depression—not just sadness, but a paralyzing listlessness, dejection, and self-pity, and an overwhelming hopelessness—over the course of life. And those episodes are beginning at earlier and earlier ages. Childhood depression, once virtually unknown (or, at least, unrecognized) is emerging as a fixture of the modern scene.[42]

That's pretty bleak. It's easy to get overwhelmed. And cynical. And despairing. And hopeless.

But God is a God of *hope*. Want proof? In Romans 15:13 Paul writes: "May the God of hope fill you with all joy and peace as you trust in him, so that you may overflow with hope by the power of the Holy Spirit." But here's the plain truth: You can't be a person of hope if you don't know what yours is. So what is your hope?

The Bible offers a powerful and hope-filled vision of how our world and lives will turn out in the end: Death gets defeated; hate staggers and falls; life wins; love muscles out on top; pain and suffering will vanish; evil and darkness are judged; faithfulness in Christ is rewarded; and God restores things to how they were originally intending to be by bringing about "a new heaven and a new earth, where righteousness dwells" (2 Peter 3:13).

Are you rooted in this kind of Big Hope? Or in something less? Maybe you just haven't thought about it. If not, I think you should. The prevailing cynicism of our times is always looking for another victim. Don't be overcome by the Age of

Melancholy. Instead, triumph in the God of hope. But you can't be a person of hope if you don't know what yours is.

ONLY GOD CAN COUNT THE APPLES IN THE SEED

A friend of mine told me about something he saw on a fridge magnet: "Anyone can count the seeds in an apple. But only God can count the apples in the seed."

The reason I share that is because it's easy to get discouraged when you don't see something important in your life bearing fruit. Maybe you've been praying about something, trying to fix a problem, or improve a situation that continually thwarts you. You look at the facts, consider the options, make a decision, act in a certain way, but don't get the results you were hoping for.

But don't get discouraged. You may be able to count the seeds in an apple, but only God can count the apples in the seed. In other words, only God can peer into the future and see the fruits of your labour—even when you can't. Just because you can't see progress doesn't mean there isn't any.

A famous verse from Deuteronomy 29:29 says, "The secret things belong to the Lord our God, but the things revealed belong to us and to our children forever, that we may follow all the words of this law." It reminds us that God can see far into a future beyond ourselves. He knows the "secret things." Our job is simply to follow the words of his law as we strive to be the hands and feet of Christ one day at a time.

Just because you can't see progress doesn't mean there isn't any. "Anyone can count the seeds in an apple. But only God can count the apples in the seed."

IF HURTS WERE HAIRS

Let's be honest. Life can hurt. There are worries, disappointments, broken dreams, challenging relationships, health problems, and pain. Max Lucado once said, "If hurts were hairs, we'd all look like grizzlies."[43]

When it comes to the challenges we face, none of us are offered a free pass; but we are promised God's presence and help through the pain. In Psalm 80:1 God is called upon as a mighty Shepherd. But then, in verses 4 and 5 we read: "How long, LORD God Almighty, will your anger smolder against the prayers of your people? You have fed them with the bread of tears; you have made them drink tears by the bowlful." Talk about passion and pain!

The whole psalm can teach us a few things about handling our hurts: First, we can know that God is a caring Shepherd. Second, we can pray to God honestly. And third, we can trust he can do something to help. Too often we hide our hurts. We believe the lie that God is a distant deity or "energy" who doesn't really care. Our prayers can be rigid and fake. And we don't really believe he's going to get involved. But Psalm 80 counsels us otherwise.

"If hurts were hairs, we'd all look like grizzlies." Well, maybe we are in fact bears; but with God, we don't need to bear our burdens alone. Know that God is a caring shepherd. Pray to God honestly. And trust that he can do something to help.

THEY WENT TO THE GUNMAN'S PARENTS' HOUSE

In October 2006, a gunman took hostages in a one-room Amish schoolhouse in Pennsylvania. He shot ten children.

One. Two. Three. Four. Five. Six. Seven. Eight. Nine. Ten. Then he shot himself. Five of the children died, and people around the world were horrified.

But get this: Just hours after it happened, people in the Amish community visited the house of the gunman's parents to express support and concern. They knew how hard it would be for them in the wake of the shootings. At the gunman's funeral, about half of those in attendance were from the Amish community. And remember, they were the victims! Again, they were in attendance to show concern, support, and to pray.

Some people in the media said it was a testament to the best within the human spirit. But to me, that kind of a comment—without taking into account the strong Christian faith of the Amish—is condescending. The Amish value, with an exceptional intensity, their relationship with God and with each other. "Be devoted to one another in love" (Romans 12:10). "Honour one another above yourselves" (Romans 12:10). "Carry each other's burdens" (Galatians 6:2). "Build each other up" (1 Thessalonians 5:11). That hurting community knew what it meant to be consistent, strong and loving in their walk with God, and they knew what it meant to be consistent, strong and loving in their walk with each other. It didn't make all their pain go away, but it helped them rise to their best in the midst of hardship.

Are you facing difficulty? If so, walk with God and walk with God's people. Journey together. It won't make all your challenges go away, but it will help you rise to your best in the midst of hardship.

THE POWER OF PERSEVERANCE

King David was able to persevere through many challenges in his life. I think he was able to do this—even through such pain and difficulty—because he was *called* by God to a godly purpose. Samuel 16 tells the story of his anointing as the future king of Israel. He knew that God has summoned him to leadership. Therefore, he was able to persevere.

Well, you are also *called* to a godly purpose. A "calling" isn't just something for King David—or for other well-known people a long time ago—but for every one who follows Jesus. In Matthew 4:17 Jesus says, "Repent, for the kingdom of heaven has come near." In other words, 'Turn away from your old life and self-centredness and make me your number one priority. God's heavenly rule of truth and love is breaking into our lives and world!' Then in Matthew 28:19-20 he gave this final commission to his disciples: "Therefore, go and make disciples of all nations, baptizing them in the name of the Father and of the Son and of the Holy Spirit, and teaching them to obey everything I have commanded you." You are *called* to a godly purpose: To be a disciple-making disciple who gets in on the ways Jesus is renovating the world with his truth, forgiveness and love. This gives God glory and you joy! And that's true no matter how old you are, what you do, or how much you've messed up.

Every relationship needs truth, forgiveness and love. Every vocation needs truth, forgiveness and love. Every plan for today or tomorrow needs truth, forgiveness and love. King David was able to persevere through many challenges in his life because he had a calling from God. Well, so can you. Because you do too. The power of perseverance isn't about taking a beating, but having a calling and being a blessing.

TRUST IN THE JUNGLE OF UNPREDICTABILITY

Life can be chaotic. And volatile. And hard. That's why friendship is so important. Christian ethicist Lewis Smedes wrote an article about the power of making a promise. He says that when you make a promise to someone, "You have created a small sanctuary of trust within the jungle of unpredictability."[44]

I think that's great advice to apply to our friendships. We make not spend every day making formal promises to our friends, but when we tell them we'll be there for them no matter what, we should honour that statement—we should be there for them no matter what. When we say they can share their burdens with us, we should share their burdens. Proverbs 18:21 says, "The tongue has the power of life and death…" That means that the words that roll off your tongue and out of your mouth can bring more life into the world—or more death. Friends need life. And friends give life.

Be a friend whose words can be trusted. This creates "a small sanctuary of trust within the jungle of unpredictability."

HOW YOU CAN EMERGE FROM THE ASHES

Who you are and who you can be emerges from the ashes of what you've been through. Hold on. Let me back up a minute.

We all have hurts. And hurts *change* us. We may not like it, but it's true. Our difficult experiences influence our attitudes and decisions. They certainly don't define us, but they become a part of us. So the question we need to ask ourselves is this: Are we going to let our hurts change us for better, or for worse?

Psalm 143 highlights how David asked God for guidance,

growth, and level ground. He trusted that God could do it, even in the midst of his many problems. After having cried out to God for mercy (verse 1) with a failing spirit (verse 7), he prayed: "Show me the way I should go, for to you I entrust my life" (verse 8). In verse 10 he continued: "Teach me to do your will... lead me on level ground." It's a helpful perspective for all of us: To let your hurts to change you for the better (and not for the worse), and to ask God for guidance, growth, and level ground, trusting that he will do it, even in the midst of your many problems.

Hurt is a part of life—but it doesn't need to be the defining part. It certainly didn't define David. And it doesn't need to define you either. That's why who you are and who you can be emerges from the ashes of what you've been through. With the right perspective, and by calling on God for help, you can emerge from the ashes of what you've been through with God's guidance, growth, and on level ground.

WHY JOY IS WISER THAN HAPPINESS

Psychologist Jonathan Haidt says that "people need adversity, setbacks, and perhaps even trauma to reach the highest levels of strength, fulfillment, and personal development."[45] I really wish that wasn't true. After all, who *wants* adversity? Who *wants* setbacks? And who *wants* trauma? Not me! But regardless of whether we *want*, many of us can personally testify to the fact that various trials have sometimes made us stronger, wiser, more resourceful, more humble, or more compassionate.

In James 1:2-3 we read, "Consider it pure joy, my brothers and sisters, whenever you face trials of many kinds, because you know that the testing of your faith produces perseverance." Again, that's a hard verse to take, especially when you're going through something tough. But the Greek word for "joy" in this verse is *chara*. It doesn't mean care-free happiness. It has to do with fixing your eyes on God, trusting in his goodness, and knowing that he will provide for you through the ups and downs of life. In this sense, joy is wiser than happiness: It has fought a few battles, gained some experience, and learned how to be steady in the wind.

Today, I want to encourage you to persevere. Pain won't persist forever. Your hurts don't have to define you. Your challenges will one day disappear in the rear view mirror. Fix your eyes on God, trust in his goodness, and know that he will provide for you through the ups and downs of life. Joy is wiser than happiness: It has fought a few battles, gained some experience, and learned how to be steady in the wind.

MESSIER'S BOLD PREDICTION—AND THE BIBLE'S

On May 25, 1994, Mark Messier did something bold. He was the captain of the New York Rangers hockey team. It was the playoffs. His team was down three games to two in the Eastern Conference finals. They had to win two games to beat their opponent, the New Jersey Devils, if they were to advance to the Stanley Cup Finals. He was very confident when he spoke to reporters: "We will win tonight." That's pretty bold! "We *will* win tonight."

When the third period started they were losing two goals to one. But then Messier scored *three* times! His prediction came true! Not only did they win the game, but they went on to win the series—and also the Stanley Cup. They became the champions.

There's a pretty bold prediction in the Bible too. 1 John 5:5 says, "Who is it that overcomes the world? Only the one who believes that Jesus is the Son of God." To "overcome the world" means to be, in the end, victorious over the powers of darkness, evil, deception and hate. They will be crushed and stomped on like an empty pop can under the foot of a bodybuilder. In their place, light, goodness, truth and love will finally and fully flourish.

If you believe that Jesus is the Son of God, that victory and inheritance will be yours! Bold predictions are just that—bold. If it was so wonderfully true for Mark Messier and the New York Rangers, how much more will it be for Christ and his people!

MAKE A PRAYER LIST

I remember a cartoon that was really funny. An unnamed man sees someone named Bob walking toward him. That triggers in his mind that he had said he would pray for Bob. But he had forgotten! So, very quietly, and as Bob quickly approaches, he whispers, "Dear God, please help Bob." Seconds later he calls out, "Hey Bob, been prayin' for ya!" It's funny. But it also reveals a truth: We have good intentions and want to pray for other people... but often forget.

So here's what you can do: *Make a prayer list*. Get a piece of paper, or open a note-taking app on your phone, and make a list. For those with poor memories or wandering minds, it can reeeeeally help! Include ongoing things to pray for like those in authority (people in government or at church), for your personal discipleship, for those you care about, for your church family, for the peace of Jerusalem, for those who are suffering —things of this nature. Also include specific people or issues you've committed to praying for, and also for decisions you're wrestling with or for God's will for this chapter of your life. That way, you won't be like the guy who said he would pray for someone (Bob), but pretty much dropped the ball.

In Colossians 4:2 Paul writes, "Devote yourselves to prayer, being watchful and thankful." The Bible tells us to pray. Jesus tells us to pray. It matters. It makes a difference. So one very practical thing you can do to up your prayer game is to make a list. Have it accessible. Use it. When you do so you're being faithful, you're being a person of your word, you're being the hands and feet of Jesus, and you're making a difference.

DEALING WITH FRUSTRATION

It's easy to get frustrated. That's why having a different attitude toward your frustrations can make them... well, less frustrating. So what is this "better approach"?

Frustrations aren't always final. They might just be calling your attention to something that needs to change. For example, if you're continually frustrated that there aren't enough hours in the day, then your frustration might be teaching you that you're too busy or over-committed. If you're continually frustrated that your devotional life is floppy, then your frustration might be teaching you that you're either misunderstanding its importance or haven't resourced yourself properly. If you're continually frustrated in a relationship, then your frustration might be teaching you that you're not communicating your feelings effectively or haven't made a proactive plan for greater relational health.

So, what are *you* frustrated about? After you've named it, ask yourself what your frustration might be teaching you. Then make a change for the better. 2 Corinthians 5:17 (NRS) says that "if anyone is in Christ, there is a new creation..." To me it's a reminder that since we have been reconciled with God, we are continually being renewed and shaped by Christ.

TURBULENCE

That's good news because I'd much rather be shaped by him than by festering frustrations!

Frustrations don't have to be final. They might just be calling your attention to something that needs to change.

THE SITUATION YOU'RE ALREADY IN

Apollo 13 was a movie starring Tom Hanks about a lunar mission that went off the rails. Remember that iconic line? "Houston, we have a problem." While in space, the three astronauts started to run out of oxygen. To help find a solution, a ground crew back on earth worked feverishly to try and design makeshift oxygen filters. Since they wouldn't be able to physically get what they made to the spaceship, they had to come up with a design that only included items that they knew the astronauts would already have on board. They didn't waste their time bemoaning their situation and all the resources they *wished* they had. Instead, they worked with what they did have to make the best of it.

That's what I think you should do. Sure, we could look at our lives (or work situation or family or church or achievements...) and whine about all the resources, people or stuff we *wished* we had. Or, we could work with what we *do* have to make the most of it. I'm not saying you shouldn't try to improve things. But what I am saying is that you shouldn't neglect what you've already been given.

Writing to the Christians in Philippi, Paul said that "God will meet all your needs according to the riches of his glory in Christ Jesus." In other words, they (and we) already have everything we need. If you are a follower of Jesus you *already* have everything you need. You have the Holy Spirit living within you, you have access to God's truth in the Bible, you have a church family, you have a purpose, and you are embraced by a heavenly Father who loves you, forgives you, provides for you, saves you and guides you!

"God will meet all your needs according to the riches of his glory in Christ Jesus." Yes, sir: The glory of his riches! So make the best of the situation you're already in.

WHY IT MATTERS THAT GOD IS GOOD

In July 2019 our church organized a jam-packed, high-energy Vacation Bible Camp. Our key verse was Psalm 106:1: "Give thanks to the LORD, for he is good; his love endures forever."

The main idea of the Camp is that God is good! Day 1: When life is *unfair*—God is good. Day 2: When life is *scary*—God is good. Day 3: When life *changes*—God is good. Day 4: When life is *sad*—God is good. Day 5: When life is *good*—God is good. I've had more than one person say that this is stuff adults need to hear as well! Definitely.

The insight that "God is good" is primarily important because it's true. God, by his very nature, can't not be good. Maybe that's obvious. But this insight is also important because it especially helps us when life is unfair, scary, changing, or sad. Why? Because you and I are not defined or hemmed-in by those situations and feelings, even though we sometimes think we are. *Dire circumstances are not death sentences.*

If we really and truly trust that God is really and truly good, we will live more confidently because we know that he is *with* us, that he is *for* us, that he is guiding us, and that he is steady—even when it's hard to see or feel. In a big ole scary world, it can make a world of a difference.

God. Is. Good.

So breathe. Trust. And walk confidently into your day

with a good God. Dire circumstances are not death sentences. A good God never stops giving new life to his children.

CONFIDENCE IS CONTAGIOUS

I was listening to a radio program called *Hockey Central at Noon* on 590 The Fan. It's a station based in Toronto, Canada. Speaking about an athlete, one of the announcers said that "confidence is contagious." It was a good point. When one person on a team is confident—not only in themselves but in the team—that attitude spreads to the other players, like a contagion.

The same is true for faith. Through the years, here's what I've discovered: People who are over-confident in themselves end up embarrassing themselves. But people who are confident in God end up boosting God's people. This doesn't mean you never have bad days. Instead, it means living with a bold certainty that *when you're by Jesus' side you're always on the winning side.*

Hebrews 13:8 nudges us on: "So we say with confidence, 'The Lord is my helper; I will not be afraid. What can mere mortals do to me?'" It's about confidence! We can be confident that God himself is our helper and that mere humans can't do anything to truly harm us. Therefore, we need not fear! Someone with that kind of confidence is contagious.

So be confident: "The Lord is my helper; I will not be afraid. What can mere mortals do to me?" When you're by Jesus' side you're always on the winning side. Not only will you actually be more confident yourself, but you'll give a boost to God's people. Confidence is contagious.

FEAR NOT, DO

Someone recently brought something to my attention. When you reverse the words "Do not fear" you get "Fear not, do." Here's why I like it.

Some people get paralyzed with fear. They sense (or create) something to be afraid of in their minds—something invisible and possibly destructive—and, as a result, cease living their lives. What I like about the "Fear not, do" reversal, is that it encourages us to push back from the mentality-of-retreat. When you step out on faith to serve God and others, and when you try to be the hands and feet of Christ— even when you don't have all the answers, and even when you don't know what the outcome might be—your fear factor goes down. Here's why: *When you actively serve God you see God act.* And that reminds you he is near, which reduces your fear.

"The LORD is the stronghold of my life—of whom shall I be afraid?" (Psalm 27:1) No one! The hands and feet of Christ are not intimidated by the invisible, destructive and unfounded fears that creep into our minds. "Fear not, do."

THE BURDEN SHIFTS TO CHRIST

Do you carry around a burden? Some invisible thing with difficulty or obligation? Maybe it's a draining responsibility that only falls to you. Maybe it's an internal and unhealthy drive to continually prove yourself to others. Or maybe it's a pile of problems you think only you can solve.

Psalm 55:22 (ESV) says, "Cast your burden on the LORD, and he will sustain you; he will never permit the righteous to be moved." In the midst of his own problems, the psalm-writer encourages us to shift the burden to God. He then connects this to the fact that God will steady us. Alone with a burden = unsteady. Casting a burden on God = steadier.

There are a few different things you can do to help make it happen: Acknowledge your burden, and also acknowledge that there are other good things in your life at the same time; pray that God take your burden onto himself; ask him to guide you through the process and to give you a wise perspective; and talk to a trusted friend for support and encouragement.

Lastly, and most importantly, ensure you've made a decision that Christ be the Lord of your life. If you think he's just a nice guy who once said some loving things, you won't trust his power or in his ability to take your burdens or direct your path. If Jesus is truly your Lord, everything changes. His muscles replace your own.

Burdens can be like rocks in your soul. But they don't need to drown you. The burden shifts to Christ when he is the Lord of your life.

THE ROAR OF THE SPIRIT

After sharing some significant insights about the Holy Spirit to his disciples, Jesus says, "Do not let your hearts be troubled and do not be afraid" (John 14:27). Why would he say that? Let me share the answer by way of a story.

In the children's movie *Pete's Dragon*, a toddler was in a car accident with his parents. Both of the parents died, but the boy somehow lived, and meandered relatively unscathed into the woods. There he was adopted by a big, green dragon! After several years, when the boy was perhaps eight or nine, he was playing near a river and saw a huge bear. But the boy, full of gusto, let out a ferocious roar with the hopes of scaring him away. At the exact same time, the dragon had sneaked out of the woods and walked up behind his young adopted friend.

From there he let out his own roar at the exact same time as the boy. The bear, seeing how outmatched he was, scampered off like a scaredy-cat into the woods! My point is this: The boy had more courage and confidence because he knew he wasn't alone; he knew that on his side he always had access to something way more powerful than himself.

Well, in Christ, so do we. If you believe in Christ, the Holy Spirit—the Person, power and presence of God—is in you. Like the boy in *Pete's Dragon*, you can have more courage and confidence because you know you aren't alone. You always have access to Someone way more powerful than you.

So boldly get involved in the work of the Holy Spirit. Honour Jesus, talk about Jesus, and do the loving work of Jesus. As you do so, trust the words of Christ, and discover for yourself how life-giving and liberating his words can be: "Do not let your hearts be troubled and do not be afraid."

COME, HOLY SPIRIT!

The church where I serve has a top-notch Youth Coordinator. Her name is Julie. Before one of our big Vacation Bible Camps she took a big white board in her office and wrote "Come, Holy Spirit!" along the bottom. Then, as the week went on, she wrote down all the different times she saw the Holy Spirit working in and through campers, volunteers, herself, and various experiences. At the end of the week, she could stand back—with a depleted sleep tank, and with sweat surely on her brow—and see how much our incredible God had been doing!

I think that when you make a point of noticing and noting how the Holy Spirit is at work, you get severely encouraged, and supremely motivated. After all, if you can look on your life and see God personally involved, it reminds you that God is personally involved! He is so loving and faithful toward us, that he works in and through us to bless, help and inspire others. In those moments Philippians 2:13 (ESV) rings true: "For it is God who works in you, both to will and to work for his good pleasure."

Are you feeling like you need a boost? If so, get a notepad or a whiteboard or open an app on your phone, and as you go through your week, take note of all the ways you see the Holy Spirit at work. I think it will leave you both encouraged and motivated. Noting when God is personally involved, makes you notice how much God is personally involved!

Come, Holy Spirit!

GOD IS ON ME!

Pastor Craig Groeschel was giving a talk at a youth camp. There was one boy who was clearly just not into it. As Craig talked, he sat there disinterested, hands in his pockets, slumped over, even looking angry. Afterwards, the young man revealed some struggles in his life. Craig asked if he could pray for him. "You can pray," he replied, "but it's not going to do any good."

In that moment, Craig felt God nudging him to pray a very bold and specific prayer: "God, I ask you in the name of your Son Jesus to reveal yourself to him now." Craig opened his eyes and the boy started shaking. "I think God is on me! I think God is on me!" he was yelling. They both fell to their knees and prayed together. In that moment, God had revealed himself powerfully to that young man. And everything changed.[46]

When we read Paul's words to "pray continually" in 1 Thessalonians 5:17, our default assumption is that it's about *duration*—about how much we pray. But what if praying continually wasn't just about how *much* we prayed but *what* we prayed. What if it was about praying through doubts, disappointments, broken dreams, desperate situations, and for a great big God to show up and show his stuff in a way we never expected? What if it was about listening for his prompts and doing what he wanted when he wanted?

One of the repeated refrains about God is that he is the "maker of heaven and earth" (Psalm 115:15, 121:2 etc). In other words, our big God does big things. You can't put him in a box. You can't tell him what to do. And you can't fully know his mind. But our big God does big things; he shoes up and shows his stuff in ways we don't expect.

You and I both know that you can't answer your own prayers. Only a big, awesome God can help. So pray big.

BEING A SPIRITUAL BILLIONAIRE

Something that robs us of our contentment is always being reminded of what others have but we don't. It has to do with envy, which Rebecca Konyndyk DeYoung describes as "feeling bitter when others have it better."[47]

Can you relate? Come on, be honest. We can sometimes feel bitter when think other people have better stuff, better experiences, better relationships, and better everything. So, what do you do?

Well, I have a theory: When you focus on what you *do* have you're less likely to be downcast by what you *don't*. Part of the problem is that in our highly consumeristic society we've been sold a dirty, thieving lie that *material* things are more important than *spiritual* things. But they're not.

In his letter to the Ephesians, Paul uses the words "riches" five times to describe what we have in Christ. Here's one of them: "God raised us up with Christ and seated us with him in the heavenly realms in Christ Jesus, in order that in the coming ages he might show the incomparable riches of his grace, expressed in his kindness to us in Christ Jesus" (Ephesians 2:6-7). I went through all five passages to make a list of the spiritual riches which we get in Christ: We are God's heirs; his riches make us special and give us a special purpose; we are the recipients of redemption, forgiveness of sin, God's generosity, and knowledge about God's will to bring harmony to all things in Jesus. We also receive hope, power, a relationship with Christ, God's kindness, love, and God living within us. Friends, in Christ, you are a spiritual billionaire!

Don't be robbed of your peace in Christ. When you focus on what you *do* have you're less likely to be downcast by what you *don't*.

SOCIAL MEDIA TORTURE = LESS CONTENTMENT

Alain de Bottom wrote a book about "status anxiety." He defined it as "a worry, so pernicious as to be capable of ruining extended stretches of our lives, that we are in danger of failing to conform to the ideals of success laid down by our society... a worry that we are currently occupying too modest a rung or are about to fall to a lower one..."[48]

And do you know what? One of the tools that the thief uses to make us feel bad compared to where we relate to others is social media. Social psychologist Ethan Kross from Michigan University said, "We measured lots and lots of other personality and behavioral dimensions... The more you used Facebook, the more your mood dropped."[49] It's where a lot of the comparisons happen. In an article titled "The Agony of Instagram," Alex Williams says that it is the "highest achievement yet in social-media voyeurism" and "a new form of torture."[50] Yikes!

Proverbs 14:30 says, "A heart at peace gives life to the body, but envy rots the bones." Would you rather have envy, comparison and rot? Or peace, life and contentment in Christ? The point is this. If you're being robbed of contentment, you may need to limit your exposure to environments that thrive on comparison. Don't scroll mindlessly. Don't buy the lie that everyone's life is always that good all the time. Don't think your status under God has anything to do with what others are up to.

If you're being robbed of contentment, you may need to limit your exposure to environments that thrive on comparison.

THEY CAN'T COMMAND THE SAME BRAIN AT THE SAME TIME

Worry. It can rob you of contentment. You know it. I know it. We all know it. Maybe that's why Jesus' words in the Sermon on the Mount are so poignant, powerful and popular: "do not worry about your life, what you will eat or drink; or about your body, what you will wear... Can any one of you by worrying add a single hour to your life?" (Matthew 6:25, 27)

In short, *worry and faith can't both command the same brain at the same time*. If we trust God to provide for our needs, and focus on seeking him, worry isn't able to get to the middle of our minds. But if we don't trust God to provide for our needs, and don't focus on seeking him, worry can quickly fill the vacuum and set up shop. Over the next few devotionals I'm going to share some thoughts about how to focus more on faith and less on worry.

This one is about rooting yourself in the voice of Christ. That means reading his words. Digesting them. Trusting them. Applying them. On a daily basis. It's so obvious that we almost miss it. This is what Jesus' listeners were doing in this very story. The more we listen to the voice of Christ, the more we trust the voice of Christ, and the more we live by faith in Christ.

There will always be volume in your life. Would you rather it be filled with the voice of Christ, or the voices of worry? So as you start to think through your battle with worry, remember that worry and faith can't both command the same brain at the same time. They might both be present, but only one can be in command. So tip the scale with step one, and root yourself in the voice of Christ. Every. Single. Day.

USE A WORRY FILTER

We're talking about the big W. Worry. Generally speaking, worry isn't good. But there are actually a few biblical passages where worry is portrayed positively.

One of them is 1 Corinthians 12:24-25 where Paul says that the various parts in the body of Christ [the church] "should have equal concern for each other." The word translated into English as "concern" is the same word Jesus uses for "worry" in Matthew 6:25-34. One of the things this teaches us is that some things are worth worrying about and some aren't. We are to be worried (concerned) for the well-being and growth of other Christians, but we should not be overly worried about material things.

With this in mind, here's something that can help you in your battle with worry. Use a filter. When you start to worry about something, use a filter to evaluate if it's worthwhile. Ask yourself, Is this a kingdom worry, or not? If it's a kingdom worry—something to do with the well-being of other Christians, or sharing Jesus' love or truth—then it's something to pay attention to. But if you're just fretting about something trivial, do your best to let it go.

Worry and faith can't both command the same brain at the same time. So use a worry filter to evaluate whether your worries are worthwhile: Is this a kingdom worry, or not?

YOU AND GRATITUDE VS. WORRY

We've been talking about worry. Unfortunately, much like water damage, friends who turn their back on you, or health problems, worries are often a difficult and deflating part of life.

To counterattack the onslaught of worry, *practice gratitude proactively*. Consider the famous Psalm 23:1: "The Lord is my shepherd, I shall not be in want." Think of that metaphor for a moment. A shepherd protects the flock from the danger of wolves and safely guides them to where they can find food and peace. God is like that Shepherd to us. Since we are prone to rabid, daily forgetfulness, we need to remind ourselves about the kind of Shepherd he is by practicing proactive gratitude. The more we remind ourselves about how much he provides for us, the less likely we are to worry incessantly about not having our needs met, being in over our heads, or destined for abject failure.

Last week I asked some people how they practiced proactive gratitude. Here are a few of their responses. A mother and daughter text each other every day saying three things they're grateful for. They've been doing it for a year and it makes a big difference. Someone else writes in a gratitude journal every morning which increases her awareness of all of her blessings. Another prays deliberately each morning and night with specific prayers of gratitude to God.

Gratitude grounds you in the ongoing goodness of God. "The Lord is my shepherd, I shall not be in want." To counterattack the onslaught of worry, practice gratitude proactively.

FOR WHEN YOU'RE STRUGGLING WITH CONTENTMENT

Psalm 62:1 is so honest: "From the ends of the earth I call to you, I call as my heart grows faint…" It reveals total desperation, and a request for help from the only One who can truly give it.

Sometimes you just don't feel great. I get it. Maybe you also feel like you're at the end of yourself with a "faint" heart. Being content or at peace can seem like a dream from another world. So I'd like to simply offer you a prayer. Why not make it your own?

Good Shepherd,
On the days when I obsess about what others have but I don't,
remind me that you have made me a spiritual billionaire in
Christ.
On the days when all I can hear is the constant comparisons to
others,
and the negative judgments, opinions and criticisms of others,
remind me that my first job is simply to be faithful to you,
and that you alone are my ultimate source of affirmation.
On the days when I drown in apathy, or when I question my
purpose,
remind me that you have called me to be salt and light,
to be useful to Jesus as his hands and feet in a hurting world,
to be proactive about attending to the needs of others.
On the days when I worry like a professional,
remind me that worry and faith can't both command the same
brain at the same time.

Remind me that you provide for my needs,
and that in you, I have everything.
In Jesus' never-failing name I pray, Amen.

WHAT YOU'VE ALREADY BEEN GIVEN

Bob Russel tells a story about a farmer who once grew discontent on his farm.[51] The lake needed to be stocked and managed and the farm itself was an incredible amount of work. It was hilly, the cows needed tending, and the fences needed mending. He decided he was unhappy and wanted to move somewhere else. So a real-estate agent came in to help him sell. The farmer showed her around, talked about his life and farm, and then the agent went away to get things ready.

A few days later she came back because she needed approval for the wording for the listing. She read the ad which described a "lovely farm in an ideal location—quiet and peaceful, contoured with rolling hills, carpeted with soft meadows, nourished by a fresh lake, and blessed with well-bred livestock." The farmer paused. He wanted her to read it to him a second time. After hearing it again he said, "I've changed my mind. I'm not going to sell. I've been looking for a place like that my whole life."

I love that story. Like the farmer, we can look around at our lot in life and only see the problems—when really, God has already given us so much, including the peace and strength he offers in Christ.

To the Philippians, Paul writes, "I have learned to be content whatever the circumstances. I know what it is to be in need, and I know what it is to have plenty. I have learned the secret of being content in any and every situation, whether well fed or hungry, whether living in plenty or in want. I can do all this through him who gives me strength" (Philippians 4:11-13). Wow.

Whoever you are, I'm sure you've got some troubles. I'm not saying you don't. But I truly believe that we often just need a change in perspective to help us see what God has already given us, including the peace and strength he offers us in Christ as we seek to give him glory.

"I have learned to be content whatever the circumstances.... I can do all this through him who gives me strength." And so can you.

A BIBLE IN 23 PIECES

In July 2007, twenty-three missionaries were held hostage by the Taliban in Afghanistan. Two of those missionaries were killed by the Taliban before the rest were released back to South Korea.

One of the survivors tells a little-known story about their time together in captivity as prisoners. On their last night together before they were separated, they figured that many, if not all of them, would be martyred for their faith. Each one of them surrendered totally to God and said they were willing to die for his glory. One of them had managed to keep a very small Bible from being confiscated. Knowing they were about to be separated, he ripped it into twenty-three different pieces, so that each of them could glace at a portion of the Bible when they needed God's strength, comfort, wisdom or hope.[52]

That's how valuable the treasure of God's word is to us. It's his message of and about Jesus—of and about his saving, healing, loving, forgiving, reconciling, and renovating work for all people. It offers us strength and comfort and wisdom and hope!

Psalm 119:105 says, "Your word is a lamp for my feet, a

light on my path." Is that true for us? Does the message of and about Jesus guide us through life's darkness and uncertainty? Is it the source of our illuminating hope? Or is it something we leave on the shelf, willingly ignore, undervalue, or take for granted?

In the Bible, not only does God teach you about who he is and what he does, but he teaches you who you are and about what he can do through you as he unceasingly breathes faithful, healing hope into a faltering, battered world.

In Luke 1:37 the angel reminds us that "no word from God will ever fail." Just because you're not held captive by the Taliban doesn't mean you need it any less.

THE OPPOSITE OF 'MISERY LOVES COMPANY'

Have you heard the expression that "misery loves company"? It's the idea that people who are miserable find some sort of comfort by being around other people who are miserable. I've also heard it used to express the idea that people who are miserable find some sort of comfort by sucking other people into their own misery.

But today I'd like to focus on something else. It is said that "misery loves company." But couldn't you rather say that *the right company heals misery*? Consider Proverbs 27:9 (NLT): "The heartfelt counsel of a friend is as sweet as perfume and incense." It doesn't say that the "never-ending misery of a friend is as sweet as perfume and incense," it says the "heartfelt counsel of a friend is as sweet as perfume and incense."

If misery loves to enlarge itself with more misery, surely heartfelt friendship enlarges itself with more heartfelt friendship. So nurture healthy, faithful friendships. They say that misery loves company. But I think the right company helps heal misery too.

※

A SIMPLE 'THANK YOU, LORD'—FROM LITTLE HOUSE TO YOURS

I remember an episode of the iconic *Little House on the Prairie*. The dad and farmer in the family was Charles Ingalls, played by Michael Landon. It was harvest time. He walked through his bountiful field, swaying his hands through his beautiful crop. As he did so he looked up and said a simple, "Thank you, Lord." Even though Charles planted the seed and did the back-breaking work, it was an acknowledgement that the harvest was really a gift from God.

Today, I want to encourage you to go through your day offering up little "Thank you, Lords" every time you see, hear or experience the blessings around you. When you're dealing with difficulty, not only are your words simple and sincere prayers to God, they're a reminder that he's continually showing blessings into your life.

An encouraging conversation... "Thank you, Lord." A beautiful tree... "Thank you, Lord." A moment of rest... "Thank you, Lord." A laugh... "Thank you, Lord." A mouthful of turkey... "Thank you, Lord." A breath of fresh air... "Thank you, Lord." A happy memory... "Thank you, Lord." A safe drive... "Thank you, Lord." A word from the Bible... "Thank you, Lord." A helping hand... "Thank you, Lord."

James 1:17 says, "Every good and perfect gift is from above, coming down from the Father of the heavenly lights, who does not change like shifting shadows." *Every* good and perfect gift is from above. Maybe that's why the ever-insightful Max Lucado says, "To reflect on your blessings is to rehearse God's accomplishments."[53]

Today, be thankful. Frequently. "Thank you, Lord."

NOT ALONE (IN THESE THREE WAYS)

Today, an assurance: You are not alone.

First, you have God's word to guide you. Think of Psalm 119:42: "I can answer anyone who taunts me, for I trust in your word." Second, you have God's Spirit to comfort you. As a Jesus-follower, God has given you this gift. In John's Gospel, the Holy Spirit is called the Comforter four times.[54] Third, you have God's people to encourage you. In 1 Thessalonians 5:11 we read, "encourage one another and build each other up…" In Hebrews 10:25 Christians are reminded to meet together for the purpose of mutual encouragement.

Going through something difficult is easier when you know you're not alone. You have God's word to guide you, God's Spirit to comfort you, and God's people to encourage you. You are not alone.

THE MODERN FOUNTAIN OF YOUTH?

Many books and movies have explored the idea of a fountain of youth—a magical flow of water that stops the aging process, and which makes you younger and feeling great. As far as we know, it doesn't exist. But one of the things I've come to discover is that a well-rested soul may be the closest thing to the fountain of youth.

The reason I include this thought in a book of devotionals called *Turbulence* is because we need rest to deal with adversity. Mental or emotional strain is still strain. And when we're not adequately rested we're not able to think clearly or creatively as we navigate the challenges we face.

One of the things I've been personally working on is rest. It doesn't come naturally to me. I have to force myself. When I get some down time my natural instinct is to do something so that I feel "productive." Maybe that's why God *commanded* rest. He actually put it in the Ten Commandments alongside not murdering or stealing. Jesus himself includes rest as one of the benefits of following him since he is the source of our strength and salvation: "Come to me, all you who are weary and burdened, and I will give you rest" (Matthew 11:28). Sign me up!

Taking time to rest isn't being lazy. It's being faithful. A well-rested soul may be the closest thing to the fountain of youth.

IN THE CHAOS

Leading up to the last Canadian federal election, I was talking to one of our church elders about the different candidates for Prime Minister. He said, 'No matter who wins, God is still in control.' He wasn't being dismissive. Elections matter. What he was doing was demonstrating great confidence in the almightiness of God.

God is on his throne. As we read in Psalm 103:19: "The LORD has established his throne in heaven, and his kingdom rules over all." It's helpful to remember this, whatever you're dealing with. When your life is in chaos, Christ is still King. When your country seems unsure, Christ is still King. When tomorrow feels uncertain, Christ is still King. When the world is ravaged by a pandemic, Christ is still King.

I'm the youngest of three brothers. When I was on the playground when I was small, I never really felt too threatened by anything. Why? Because somewhere nearby, I always had two big brothers hanging around. The same idea is true with God—but sooooo much more. When you know that God is in control, you're less likely to agonize when you're not. Take heart. In the chaos, Christ is still King.

WHEN YOU CANNOT DIRECT THE WINDS

When people go through a tough time in life, they sometimes lash out at the people they care about most. After a hard day, in a period of anxious uncertainty, or during a year of gut-wrenching decision-making, we can blame, shame or yell at the people in our own boat—after all, they're the ones close enough to be in the line of fire at day's end. But just because someone is beside you in the storms of life, that doesn't mean they're to blame.

None of us are perfect. And sure, we all have things we need to work on. But consider what Paul says in Romans 12:10: "Honor one another above yourselves." To honour someone is to respect them, to acknowledge their value and contribution. The same goes for those we love, even when we don't feel like being loving.

When people go through a tough time in life, they sometimes lash out at the people they care about most, people in their own ship, so to speak. But is it wise to do battle with members of your own crew? As Thomas More wisely said more than 500 years ago, "Don't give up the ship in a storm because you cannot direct the winds."[55]

"Honor one another above yourselves."

NEIL ARMSTRONG... AND JESUS

I once read a story about an elementary school class who was learning about the moon. They wondered, 'What does zero-gravity feel like?' and 'What did it really look like out there?' As a surprise, the teacher had arranged for none other than Neil Armstrong to make a special appearance! In the middle of their discussion, in he walked. All of a sudden, their text books didn't matter. They could talk directly with an expert, the first man to walk on the moon. He was the ultimate authority on the subject!

In a similar way, Jesus is our ultimate authority on the subject of finding peace with God, and furthering peace between people. Colossians 1:19 says, "For God was pleased to have all his fullness dwell in him [Jesus]..." Think of that for a minute. If God was pleased to have *all* his *fullness* dwell in Jesus, there's no greater expert than him!

If we truly know Jesus, we'll know true peace.

I believe that so much of the pain in our world, the uncertainty in our world, and the fear in our world, would be helped if we could be confident about our source of peace—not only for our relationship with God, but for our relationship with one another.

We can be. Jesus' identity, love, truth, integrity and example make him our ultimate authority. If Neil Armstrong was supremely qualified to talk about what it was like on the moon, how much more qualified is Jesus to talk about peace with God, and peace between people.

In a troubled world, be confident in Christ, the "Prince of Peace" (Isaiah 9:6). If we truly know Jesus, we'll know true peace.

A FROG IN YOUR HEART

I was visiting a woman in a nursing home. She has aches and pains. She's had more than her share of heartache. Through it all she's had an enduring faith in Jesus.

On this particular visit, she told me her outlook on life: F.R.O.G. Um, pardon? Then she explained it: "Through every stage of life I've had to remind myself to FROG: Fully Rely On God." Aha! She had come to know and trust the God "who is able to do immeasurably more than all we ask or imagine…" (Ephesians 3:20).

Today, this week, this month, this year, every year… I encourage you to FROG. To help with this, here's what you can do: (1) truly trust in God's presence, power and provision, and (2) spend less time fretting about things in the future you can't control. Easy, right? Not always. If it was easy everyone would already be doing it! But ours is a God of love "who is able to do immeasurably more than all we ask or imagine."

You may not always have a frog in your throat, but you can have FROG in your heart. (Sorry, couldn't help myself.) Truly trust in God's presence, power and provision, and spend less time fretting about things in the future you can't control.

TAKE THE WORD WITH YOU

Today I'd like to offer a very practical, super-simple, down-to-earth, easy-peasy, knock-it-out-of-the-park idea: Take your Bible with you. Let me explain.

Followers of Jesus think the Bible is very important. It's the primary place where we learn about God's will and wisdom for our lives. Many of us hold the conviction—as I hope you do—that the more you get into God's word, the more God's word gets into you.

But some of the people I talk to get into a rut. Or they get tired. Or lazy. Or busy. Or distracted. They start each day two steps behind and end the day exhausted. We know we should read our Bibles every day—but struggle. I get it. That's why you should take your Bible with you as you go about your day. Maybe it's a smaller Bible that you have, or just a New Testament. Maybe it's the free app on your phone from *YouVersion*.

Recently I was in the doctor's waiting room. So I pulled out my Bible. Maybe you have a few extra minutes over the lunch hour. Instead of going online and getting frustrated because of the thoughtless and insane things people say and post, why not open your Bible for a few minutes? Maybe it's while waiting for the bus, or for your kid to finish swimming lessons.

Psalm 119:105 says, "Your word is a lamp for my feet, a light on my path." But not if we keep it shut. Take the word with you.

GOD'S GRIP ON YOU—KIND OF LIKE A SLEEPWALKING ROPE

No matter how often we're told otherwise, it's easy to slip back into the thinking that God only loves us if we do a really, really good job of loving him back. All the time. 'If we're really bad,' we think, 'he won't forgive us.' 'If we miss the mark, have an off day (or year), or blow our second, third or fourth chance,' we think, 'he'll stop caring.'

But being "in Christ" is not a fickle affair. It's a phrase Paul uses many times in the Bible. One example is Romans 8:1 where he says that "there is now no condemnation for those who are in Christ Jesus..." No condemnation. In Christ, we are enveloped, surrounded, and embraced by the love of a God whose grip on us is thoroughly stronger that our grip on him.

When I was young, my brother Jason started to sleepwalk. It didn't happen *all* the time, but it certainly happened *some* of the time. So when he and my dad went on a camping trip out into the deep woods, it was obviously a concern. To ensure my brother didn't sleepily wander out of their tent and get lost in the middle of the night, my dad tied a rope from his ankle to my brother's ankle before they went asleep. They were bound together.

So it is when you are "in Christ." You are secure. God's grip on you is greater than your grip on him.

MARANA THA

I want to share a short, special prayer with you so that you can include it in your daily arsenal. When you're on your knees, or not. When you're driving, or walking. When you're calm, or fed up. When you're composed, or frazzled. It's biblical, easy to memorize, and powerful.

"Marana Tha."

It's Aramaic (the language Jesus spoke) and means "Our Lord, come." Paul tells it to us in 1 Corinthians 16:22 and offers no explanation. To me that probably means it was so widely known—at least in Corinth—that he didn't have to. Everyone knew what he was talking about and what it meant.

When we pray "Marana Tha," I think we pray for at least two things: First, we pray for Jesus to return and bring an end to pain, tears, sin, estrangement and brokenness, and replace it with "a new heaven and a new earth, where righteousness dwells" (2 Peter 3:13). Sounds amazing! Second, we pray that Jesus come powerfully into the specific situations, thoughts and contours of our day. All that in two words? Yes!

No matter who we are or what we're going through, all of us need the powerful presence of God, don't we? *Marana Tha.*

PESSIMISM & OPTIMISM VS. REALITY

There was a family with two boys. One was an extreme pessimist. The other was an extreme optimist. The parents didn't like their extreme attitudes, so they tried a gift-giving experiment at Christmas to try and correct them. They thought that if they gave the pessimist a gift that was so over-the-moon awesome, he would simply have to be happy. They gave him the latest iPhone. But he just frowned: 'Dumb thing is probably gonna break.'

Next was the gift for the optimistic boy. He was always so happy about everything that they wanted to get him something so bad that he would simply have to feel sour about. That way, he would learn a valuable lesson about disappointment. He opened his gift, only to find a pile of manure. It stunk up the whole room! But instead of a frown, a huge smile came across his face. 'Why are you happy?' his parents asked, 'You got manure!' 'I know, I know,' he said excitedly, 'that means there has to be a pony around here somewhere!'[56] Talk about optimism!

Both boys had unhelpful perspectives: one so negative that it was out-of-touch with reality, and the other so positive that it was out-of-touch with reality. How often do we do the same? We think the sky is falling when it isn't. Or we put our hope in the wrong things which lead to disappointment. The antidote to naïve optimism and sky-is-falling pessimism is *reality*.

In 2 Corinthians 4:16 Paul reminds us about our reality: "we do not lose heart. Though outwardly we are wasting away, yet inwardly we are being renewed day by day." Though we live in frail bodies in a sin-soaked world, we are being renewed on a daily basis by the power of God. In the very next verse he writes, "For our light and momentary troubles are achieving for us an eternal glory that far outweighs them all." Life is tough. God is good. He is with you. Forever.

Do you let naïve optimism or sky-is-falling pessimism take over your brain? The antidote to naïve optimism and sky-is-falling pessimism is reality. Life is tough. God is good. He is with you. Forever.

FOUR WAYS TO DRAW CLOSER TO GOD

James 4:8 says, "Come near to God and he will come near to you." When we cultivate a closer relationship with God, we experience his power and presence more and more. In short, *the closer God is the more courage there is.*

Consider the example of Mary. In her famous song of praise in Luke 1:46-55, she shows how she is close to God in at least four ways: First, she believes in the personal God of the Bible (verses 48-9), not some distant deity who isn't really involved or concerned with daily life. Second, she knows the Scriptures (verse 55). How else would she know what God had "promised our ancestors"? Third, she has faith, even when it's risky. She had a controversial pregnancy, which could have threatened her life and the well-being of her family. Her life in a broader sense was far from easy. And then she watched the torture and cruel crucifixion of her son. Through it all, she was faithful. Fourth, she is humble (verses 48, 52). Her posture is one of simple servant-hood where loyalty to God is foremost. These qualities helped Mary to be close to God, and to have courage as a result.

So, do you want to draw near to God? If so, maybe you can learn from Mary. Look at the following list, and honestly ask yourself which you need to work on: (1) Believing in the personal God of the Bible (instead of some distant deity); (2) knowing the Scriptures, instead of just guessing at what God's will is; (3) having faith, even when it's risky, instead of always staying in the comfort zone; (4) being humble, instead of being selfish and just living for you.

"Come near to God and he will come near to you."

THE DAWN OF GOD

Glimmers of hope are handles to hold when you fear you might topple over in the turbulence of life.

One of those glimmers of hope is found in Psalm 130:5-6: "I wait for the LORD, my whole being waits, and in his word I put my hope. I wait for the Lord more than watchmen wait for the morning, more than watchmen wait for the morning."

First, God's word is a source of hope. Read it. Digest it. Let it nourish you. Daily. Second, the night doesn't last forever. Morning comes. "More than watchmen wait for the morning."

Pierre Teilhard de Chardin, the French philosopher and priest, said: "In the shadow of death may we not look back to the past, but seek in utter darkness the dawn of God."[57]

The dawn of God!

Night doesn't last for ever. God's dawn will come—and *is* coming! Have hope.

IN OUR WEAKNESS THAT STRENGTH GOES VIRAL

There's an expression that drives me nuts: 'God helps those who help themselves.' (No, it's not from the Bible.) Even though it's true that God helps those who help themselves, he doesn't *only* help those who help themselves. He also helps the down and out and those who are chasing their tails.

In Romans 8:26 and 27 Paul writes, "the Spirit helps us in our weakness. We do not know what we ought to pray for, but the Spirit himself intercedes for us through wordless groans... the Spirit intercedes for God's people in accordance with the will of God." God helps us "in our weakness." Even when we don't know "what we ought to pray for" the Holy Spirit continues to intercede "for us through wordless groans." And he does so in a way that honours his own will. Talk about a loving and understanding God! He advocates for you—even when you're a bumbling mess who is too exhausted or hurting to think straight.

In his book *The End of Me*, Kyle Idleman says, "God is always strong, but in our weakness that strength goes viral."[58] In and through our weakness, when our masks are removed, and when our guards are down, and when the illusion of our own self-sufficiency is shattered into a thousand pieces, God continues to work.

Take the pressure out of your prayers. Be honest. And ask for the Spirit to help you, even when you can't stammer a single sentence together. Our lives are built not on what we can do, but on what God can do. "God is always strong, but in our weakness that strength goes viral."

A WORSHIP STATE OF MIND

Today, let's worship God. 'But Matthew, it's not Sunday.' Well, yes—you're right. It's not. But worship is an all-the-time thing, not just a some-of-the-time thing. Theologian John Piper writes that "worship means consciously knowing and treasuring and showing the supreme worth and beauty of God."[59] Oh yes.

While there is something special that happens on the first day of the week when God's people gather to honour and praise him, worship is also a broader mode of being, a state of mind. It's what lies behind Paul's words in Romans 12:1-2: "I urge you, brothers and sisters, in view of God's mercy, to offer your bodies as a living sacrifice, holy and pleasing to God—this is your true and proper worship. Do not conform to the pattern of this world, but be transformed by the renewing of your mind."

Look around you—at the trees, at the birds, at the people. Look within you—at your design, at your heart, at your purpose. No matter what you're doing, worship our incredible Creator God, who continues to breathe life into our world, and who continues to make all things new because of his great, majestic love. In this crazy, mixed-up world, we need the reminder, don't we?

As Piper reminds us, "worship means consciously knowing and treasuring and showing the supreme worth and beauty of God." Worship doesn't just happen at a certain time—it's a state of mind.

OUR STRENGTH EVERY MORNING

Dick and Rick are members of Team Hoyt. Together they've competed in sixty-four marathons, two hundred and six triathlons at Ironman distance, and two hundred and four 10K runs. In total, that's over six thousand kilometres!

But get this. Dick, the father, can run. But Rick, the son, isn't able to run *or* speak. It's been that way since he was born. The medical team didn't give him much hope. But his parents did. They took care of him and, as he grew, knew he was bright. He enrolled in school, and eventually earned a college degree.

When Rick was fifteen he asked his father if he could enter a five-mile charity race. So his dad rigged up a three-wheeled wheelchair and they entered *together*. With that, Team Hoyt was launched. They're both in the race, but Rick needs to totally rely on the strength of his father.[60]

So do we. We need to totally rely on the strength of our *heavenly* Father. Isaiah says it with honesty and clarity: "Lord, be gracious to us; we long for you. Be *our strength* every morning, our salvation in time of distress" (Isaiah 33:2, emphasis added).

It's not all up to you. You are tethered to a strong, strong God. You benefit from his light. And you are guided forward by his words. In him, you may fall, but he will lift you up. You may get a bit lost, but it will only be temporary. You may get a bit low, but then you will hear his encouraging words embracing your soul.

Talk to him. Listen to his word. Spend time with him. Spend time with his people. Love the ones he loves. And rest in the strength that only he can give. After all, he's your perfect Father. "Lord, be gracious to us; we long for you. Be *our strength* every morning, our salvation in time of distress."

MY SHEEP LISTEN TO MY VOICE

A group of young people saw a downhill skier going down the hill with someone else super-close behind them. The skier in the front was an instructor. They were yelling instructions to the person behind: "Left, right, straight, right." Thinking it would be funny to mess them up, the youth started calling out their own set of instructions. They figured they could throw them off by confusing the person in the back! But the two skiers were unfazed. The one behind continued to do exactly what the instructor was saying. When the skiers got closer they realized something and became embarrassed. They could see a sign on the chest of the person in the back: "Blind Skier."[61]

You're right. They shouldn't have done it. But the story illustrates something significant. The blind skier was able to tune out the other distracting voices which were trying to throw him off course. We need to do the same thing: tune out the distracting voices which are trying to throw us off course.

In John 10:27 Jesus says, "My sheep listen to my voice; I know them, and they follow me." Do you have a decision to make? A direction to choose? A priority to set? Are you struggling through the current chapter of your life and aren't sure where to turn or who to listen to? Do your best to learn what Jesus teaches and act accordingly. Don't get distracted by the dozens of other voices which have a remarkable tendency to try and throw you off course.

TO HELP US PILOT OUR LIVES

Have you ever wanted to some wisdom or direction for something you're dealing with? You've prayed—but still aren't sure what to do. You've read the Bible—but still aren't sure what to do. You've fasted—but still aren't sure what to do. In these situations, God is so merciful to us. He puts people in our lives to help us pilot our lives! But how do we know who these people are?

In Philippians, Paul explains that we can look to the example of others: "Join together in following my example, brothers and sisters, and just as you have us as a model, keep your eyes on those who live as we do" (3:17). More specifically, he holds up Timothy as an example. But what makes him so mature and commendable? One of the character traits Paul mentions is Timothy's genuine concern for the welfare of others (Philippians 3:20).

In light of this, we can also seek out mature Christians who have a genuine concern for the welfare of others. In turn, they may be great sources of wisdom for what we ourselves are dealing with. Think of someone in your own life who has a genuine concern for the welfare of others. They might be someone God has put in your life to give you help and hope for the uncertainty and ambiguity you're facing.

Seek them out. Be honest. Prayerfully ask for wisdom. God puts people in our lives to help us pilot our lives.

PRAYING FOR 'LITTLE THINGS'

In Philippians 4:6-7, Paul writes: "Do not be anxious about anything, but in every situation, by prayer and petition, with thanksgiving, present your requests to God. And the peace of God, which transcends all understanding, will guard your hearts and your minds in Christ Jesus."

Sometimes we think that God only wants to hear about the *big* things we're dealing with—things like life-altering decisions, the strength to battle an illness, the big risks of faith, and the emergencies. It's as if we think God doesn't want to be bothered by the normal, everyday details of our Joe Blow lives. But Paul says we should pray "in every situation."

Pray to God about your midterms, about how tired you are, about your pesky co-worker, about how you feel about your body image, about your weekend, about your credit card bill, about your... well, you get the picture. Pray for the little things. When you pray for little things big things happen. Here's an example that Paul specifically mentions: "And the peace of God, which transcends all understanding, will guard your hearts and your minds in Christ Jesus."

God guards the hearts and minds of those who give him their hearts and minds. Don't be timid or embarrassed. The One you're talking to made you. Pray for the little things.

GOING THUD ON THE METAPHORICAL GROUND

I once heard a story about a 5-year old boy who lived on a farm. His parents were harsh, especially his father. It was a brick farm house with a large porch that wrapped around the front. In those days there weren't always railings so children had to be careful, especially since it was about five feet off the ground.

One day the boy was standing at the edge of the porch looking down. His father walked over and held out his arms, as if to say, 'Jump! I'll catch you!' This little boy gladly jumped, as if to land happily in his father's arms. But while he was in the air, his father pulled his arms back, letting the boy crash to the ground. Thud. The mother ran over to her crying son. She looked to her husband for an explanation. He looked down at his son and said: "Life is hard. People are going to let you down. And you have to learn to not trust people, so the sooner you learn that lesson, the better."

I hope none of us have had that experience. But as we go through life, difficult experiences do happen to us—a harsh word, a betrayal, a searing disappointment—and we go thud on the metaphorical ground. Our experiences can harden us, and we lose something of the child within each one of us.

Jesus tells his disciples that "unless you change and become like little children, you will never enter the kingdom of heaven" (Matthew 18:3). But what is it about little children that is so commendable? One of the traits he highlights is quite simply that they "believe" in him (Matthew 18:6). To believe in Jesus is to wholeheartedly trust and depend on him. To wholeheartedly trust that his words are true and are the best for you. And to wholeheartedly depend on his love, wisdom and strength instead of your own.

Have your experiences hardened you? Have you lost something of the child within? Trust God. Live in dependence on him. Wholeheartedly. Unlike the father in the story, our Heavenly Father is perfect in his love for us. As we are reminded in Deuteronomy 33:27: "The eternal God is your refuge, and underneath are the everlasting arms." Because of that he will never let us fall.

WHEN THERE ARE BARKING DOGS ALL AROUND YOU

A high school basketball team was behind by one point with just seconds left in the game. So they came up with a clever play. They had possession of the ball. When the referee blew the whistle to resume play, they threw the ball inbounds to a player close to the basket. But at the exact same time, all the other players immediately dropped to their knees and started barking like dogs, loudly! The defending team was so surprised that they just stood there, stunned. As a result, the player with the ball—who was standing unguarded right beside the basket—easily scored the basket and got the two points. They pulled ahead to win the game.[62] You've got to admit that it was pretty clever.

Is it just me, or is this kind of like the world we live in? There can be so much crazy distraction—so many 'barking dogs,' so to speak—that we just stand around baffled, not sure what to do. As a result, we can miss the life God invites us to live because we've been bamboozled by a hurricane of advertising, envy, busyness, and social media distraction.

In light of all this, the author of Psalm 119 has a liberating and correcting perspective: "I will meditate on your precepts and fix my eyes on your ways" (Psalm 119:15, ESV). When we meditate on God's precepts and fix our eyes on his ways, we start to immunize ourselves against the illness of unworthy distractions.

So today, ask yourself this: Am I pursuing God's ways—or unworthy distractions? Life is short. In the scope of eternity, you only have seconds left. And there are barking dogs all around you. Choose well. "I will meditate on your precepts and fix my eyes on your ways."

※

SUPER-CONQUERORS

If you're a follower of Christ you're a "super-conqueror." Did you know that? Do you feel like it? Do you need some convincing?

In Romans 8:37 Paul writes: "No, in all these things we are more than conquerors through him who loved us." The words "we are more than conquerors" translate a Greek word meaning, quite literally, *hyper-conquerors*, or *super-conquerors*. But the meaning is lost if we miss what comes next: "through him who loved us." Jesus is the ultimate conqueror. Through his life, death, crucifixion and resurrection, he has won the victory over death, evil, sin, Satan and darkness.

But that's not all. It's a *vicarious* victory. What *he* does benefits those who are a part of his family, clan or tribe—and that's us! In this sense, we are *coattail conquers*. We are victorious in life and death, not because of what we have done, but because of what Christ has done for us. By faith, we get to ride his coattails in the biggest victory parade the world has ever known!

Early in 2020 we learned the horrific news about the beheading of the Rev. Lawan Andimi, a Nigerian pastor who was killed by Boko Haram extremists. The headline at ChristianPost.com read, "Nigerian pastor who praised God in ransom video beheaded after refusing to deny Christ." Do you think Rev. Andimi was defeated? Absolutely not. He was—and is—a coattail conqueror, un-threatened and un-intimidated by the evil powers who can threaten the body but not the soul.

You too, are a coattail conqueror. Live with humble confidence as the champion Christ has made you to be. "No, in all these things we are more than conquerors through him who loved us."

DO YOU EXPECT TO HEAR FROM GOD?

Do you want to hear from God? Me too. Maybe you want to hear God's voice to help you with a tough decision, through a challenging season of life, or to give you some encouragement. Whatever the reason, I truly believe that *you're less likely to hear God speaking to you if you never expect him to.*

In the parable of the sower, Jesus said, "Whoever has ears to hear, let them hear" (Mark 4:9). One of the things this teaches us is that it's possible to hear something but still not truly hear it.

I think God is communicating to us all the time. Unfortunately, a lot of people think that God isn't speaking to them unless they hear an audible voice. But God speaks to his people in a variety of ways. Yes, sometimes there is an audible voice. But more often than not, it's through different means.

One of them is *worship*. That's when God's people gather to sing, pray, read the Bible, learn, and encourage one another. It can happen in a shared building, but it can also happen in our homes. We have discovered how true that is during the COVID-19 pandemic.

Consider Acts 13:3: "While they were worshiping the Lord and fasting, the Holy Spirit said, "Set apart for me Barnabas and Saul for the work to which I have called them." While they were worshiping, God spoke.

Leonard Sweet and Frank Viola write, "When we enter a spirit of loving worship through singing or spoken praise, our spirits become more sensitive to hear Jesus speak as well as to receive from Him. In doing so, we turn *off* our souls to the frequencies of the world, turn them *on* to the spiritual realm, and tune them *in* to hear the voice of our Lord."[63]

As you go through your week, and as you worship God, or prepare to worship God, ask him to use that experience to communicate with you. Ask him to give you "ears to hear."

You're less likely to hear God speaking to you if you never expect him to.

SLAUGHTER UNTRUE THOUGHTS WITH TRUTH

Many of us face battles. More often than we'd like. And many of those battles begin in the mind. But you can respond swiftly and firmly by slaughtering untrue thoughts with truth as soon as they enter your brain. That truth is, in the words of Paul in Romans 8:37, that "in all these things we are more than conquerors through him who loved us."

For example, here's an untrue thought that can go on the offensive. "The difficulty you're going through is because God doesn't care!" Maybe it's something someone said to you, or that you've said to yourself. Or maybe it's from the Evil One himself. After all, in John 8:44 Jesus calls him the "father of lies." Based on Romans 8:37, here's an immediate response: "No, I am more than a conqueror through him who loved me."

Here are a few more examples. Untrue thought: "You're not good enough, or smart enough, or pretty enough, or handsome enough, or strong enough, or popular enough!"

Response: "No, I am more than a conqueror through him who loved me." Untrue thought: "You're such a loser. Nothing is ever going to get better!" Response: "No, I am more than a conqueror through him who loved me."

Don't confuse this with "the power of positive thinking." That has nothing to do with it—although, to be sure, what I'm suggesting is definitely positive. What I'm talking about here is standing firm on biblical truth.

Many of the battles we face begin with the battle of the mind. Don't relinquish a single, solitary inch. Slaughter untrue thoughts with truth.

THE WORD SHE WROTE ACROSS HER CHEST

Here is one of Paul's prayers for the Ephesians: "I pray that the eyes of your heart may be enlightened in order that you may know the hope to which he has called you, the riches of his glorious inheritance in his holy people, and his incomparably great power for us who believe" (Ephesians 1:18-19).

Margaret Feinberg is a teacher and writer who was diagnosed with breast cancer. In the midst of her difficulty she decided to adopt a strategy: To fight back with joy. On her first visit to a possible oncologist, she surprised the doctor with something unique. Before she put on her hospital gown, she wrote a single word across her chest. It was a kind of litmus test to see whether or not the doctor would be a good fit for her personality and for her approach. But it was also meant to remind both of them, in a joyful way, of the big picture. What was that word?

"Victory!"[64]

What are you dealing with? Broken dreams? The death of Plan A? Family problems? Health problems? Mental health challenges? Friend problems? Career problems? Money problems? Frustration? Feeling different because of your faith? A past that won't stop haunting you? Consequences of bad decisions? Guilt? Loneliness? All of the above?

Remember the big picture: In Christ, the victory is yours! "I pray that the eyes of your heart may be enlightened in order that you may know the hope to which he has called you, the riches of his glorious inheritance in his holy people, and his incomparably great power for us who believe."

Don't be afraid to laugh in the face of hardship—and to fight back with the joy of knowing and trusting Jesus.

NOT MADE OF STUFF THAT SINKS

Speaking to his disciples, Jesus said: "I will ask the Father, and he will give you another advocate to help you and be with you forever—the Spirit of truth... you know him, for he lives with you and will be in you" (John 14:16-17).

There was a cork who was having a great time just bobbing up and down in the ocean. But a whale came along and decided he was going to have some fun with the cork. So he pounded him down into the water with his massive tail. Splash! The cork went way down into the water, swirled around for a bit, but then came back up. After all, corks float. But the whale wasn't satisfied. He really wanted to mess with the cork. So he swam toward him at great speed, jumped out of the water, and came crashing down on the cork belly first. The cork plunged way down into the water, even further than before. He swirled around in the current a little bit, made his way through some bubbles, and came back up. This upset the whale. So he got another one of his big whale friends, and together they swam toward the cork from opposite directions, jumped out of the water at the same time, and came down together on the cork, side by side, sandwiching him, plunging him even further toward the bottom of the ocean. The cork went waaaay down, swirled around in the depths of the ocean, but eventually floated back to the surface. The cork looked over at the whales and said, "You might as well give up. I'm not made of stuff that sinks."[65]

Well, if you're a follower of Christ, neither are you. People may try to get you down. Insult you. Criticize you. Mess with you. Threaten you. But God is with you. In Christ you have love, forgiveness, salvation and purpose. Plus, the Holy Spirit is in you!

Today, fear not. You are not made of stuff that sinks.

SAVIOUR?

An air force pilot told Max Lucado about the time he forgot to put on his own seat belt. He went through all the other checklists, but he forgot to do up his belt. His jet was designed in such a way that after it took off he couldn't buckle up after the fact. So if something went wrong mid-flight and he had to hit the eject button, the parachute would be attached to his seat—but not to him! He would have turned into a human projectile. Lucado offers this comment: "Can you imagine flying a jet without a parachute? Many do."[66]

This story is meant to bring into focus the distinct role of Jesus as *Saviour*. He offers us something life-preserving and life-giving without which we don't stand a chance. Many of us mentally acknowledge this. But do we really live like its true? Do we just say Jesus is our Saviour for what he offers us in the next life, or also for this one? Do we say it because it's a doctrinally correct statement, or also because we truly need his strength? Do we say it because we agree with his loving purpose, or also because we need his loving purpose for our lives?

When I say that Jesus is my Saviour, I'm saying that yes, without him I'm hell-bound. But I'm also saying that *his* plan for my life is better than *my* plan for my life; that *his* strength is better than *my* strength; that *his* loving purpose for my life is greater than anything I can cobble together on my own.

1 John 4:14-16 says: "And we have seen and testify that the Father has sent his Son to be the Savior of the world. If anyone acknowledges that Jesus is the Son of God, God lives in them and they in God. And so we know and rely on the love God has for us."

Rely.

Since we are belted securely in the plane of life, we can live each new day with a peace, passion and purpose that we could never muster on our own, flying in the light of the Son.

Even in turbulence.

'A RECESS PROBLEM' BY SARAH RUTTAN

A POSTSCRIPT FROM AN ELEVEN-YEAR OLD CHRISTIAN

INTRODUCTION

Most of the time it's easy to be a Christian. People know me to be a Christian. They know what I stand for and what I don't. But sometimes I am put in a situation that will either make me hurt someone's feelings and get it my way, or choose the Christian way and not necessarily what I wanted at first. I will illustrate this with a skit.

Let's say a kid who is not so popular asked to play with your group of friends. Your friends give you the choice about what to do. (Thanks a lot, guys!) Depending on what you decide, you are going to either hurt this kid's feelings and leave them alone for that recess, or choose the Christian way and try to include them. Of course, you should always choose the Christian way. So you should let the kid play with you.

Your friends might get upset with you, but if they are truly your great forever friends, they will understand. I once heard that if you have one or two good friends you are very blessed. So if you have one or two great friends to stick by your side, you are doing great!

TOUGH SITUATIONS

If you are put in a situation like the one I already talked about, and if for some reason you need to refuse to play with them—maybe because they do disrespectful things and are mean even after you are patient and give them many chances—here are some ways to refuse without hurting their feelings.

First, try to explain why they can't play with you. Explain reasonably why they've upset you. Your main goal is to not hurt them but still get your point across. For example, you could say, 'I'm sorry but you haven't been very kind to us. We've given you lots of chances but you haven't stopped.' Then they might walk away or get mad with you. If they get mad at you it's good to see how mad they really are on a scale from one to ten, with one being not-very-mad (like glaring at you and then walking away), and ten being an out-of-control tantrum. You don't want to get hurt. So in the situation of a level-10 tantrum, go get an adult with authority. In times like that I also always like to say a prayer for the situation and to know that God is with you.

Second, you should always explain. Explaining is always the way to go! That way, the person knows what they did to upset you. But then, if the person starts apologizing to everyone sincerely, and asks to be forgiven, then you always answer Yes. You were forgiven for all your sins when Jesus died on the cross, so you should always forgive those who have done wrong against you. In The Lord's Prayer it says, 'forgive us our trespasses as we forgive those who trespass against us.' So we must always forgive no matter what that person has done. If they repent they must be forgiven and given another chance to play with you.

Third and finally, this is the most hard of all. If someone was mean in the past and asks to be forgiven, you will forgive them. But if that person asks to be forgiven every day, but does not mean it and does not repent, then you can say no to them.

This might make them sad, but if they don't *truly* ask to be forgiven or repent, their sorry isn't honest.

CONCLUSION

These ways of dealing with a difficult situation like this without hurting someone's feelings was based on this idea: You live not to your gain; you live not for others' happiness; you live for the Christian thing to do.

> *This has been A Recess Problem, written by Sarah Ruttan, an 11 year old Christian and daughter of Matthew Ruttan.*
>
> *Thank you for reading! And God bless you!*

REFERENCES AND NOTES

TURBULENCE

1. As noted in: Max Lucado, *Fearless: Imagine Your Life Without Fear* (Nashville: Thomas Nelson, 2009), 5.
2. *Overcomer* was a movie produced by Alex, Stephen, and Shannon Kendrick, and released in 2019 by Sony Pictures. See www.OvercomerMovie.com.
3. Thomas More, *A Dialogue of Comfort Against Tribulation*, ed. Terri Ann Geus (Mineola: Dover, 2016), 237.
4. Richard E. Byrd, *Alone* (GP Putnam's Sons, Inc., 1938), 19.
5. Billy Graham, *Nearing Home* (Nashville: Thomas Nelson, 2011), 131-2.
6. For this devotional I want to acknowledge Dr. Jordan Peterson who, in an interview with *Weekend Sunrise* in Australia in June 2018, said: "you need a meaning in your life to offset the suffering in your life." This idea is related to what I say in today's devotional.
7. Karl Barth, *Prayer and Preaching* (London: SCM Press, 1964), 16.
8. As told in: Mark Batterson, *The Grave Robber: How Jesus Can Make Your Impossible Possible* (Grand Rapids: Baker Books, 2014), 156-7.
9. Jud Wilhite, *The God of Yes: How Faith Makes All Things New* (New York: Faith Words, 2014), 128.
10. Christian Keysers, "Mirror Neurons: Are We Ethical By Nature?" in Max Brockman, ed., *What's Next? Dispatches on the Future of Science* (New York: Vintage, 2009), 23.
11. Dietrich Bonhoefer, *Letters & Papers from Prison* (London: SCM Press, 1953), 122.
12. John C. Lennox, *Where is God in a Coronavirus World?* (The Good Book Company, 2020), 44.
13. As quoted in: "God shouts to us in our pain" by Daniel Ritchie (January 16, 2017). Accessed at https://www.desiringgod.org/articles/god-shouts-to-us-in-our-pain
14. Thomas More, *A Dialogue Comfort Against Tribulation*, ed. Terri Ann Geus (Mineola: Dover, 2016), 60.
15. I recall this quote from John Ortberg, pastor at Menlo Church, California, but cannot find the source. Learn more at: http://www.johnortberg.com/
16. Frederick Buechner, *Telling Secrets* (New York: HarperSanFrancisco, 1991), 49.
17. I read about this experiment by Jonathan Haidt in: Kyle Idleman, *Aha:*

REFERENCES AND NOTES

   Awakening. Honesty. Action. (Colorado Springs: David C Cook, 2014), 51-53.
18. As told in: Max Lucado, *Cure for the Common Life: Living in Your Sweet Spot* (Nashville: W Publishing Group, 2005), 93-94.
19. Martin Luther (1483-1546); translation, Frederick H. Hedge (1805-1890); v.3, Omer Westendorf (1916-). Words: v.3, copyright © World Library Publications, 1964, a division of J.S. Paluch Company, Inc.
20. William J. Broad, "Scientists' New Findings Link Titanic's Fast Sinking to Rivets," *San Antonio Express-News*, April 15, 2008.
21. The article was published on May 6, 2020 and can be read at https://ca.thegospelcoalition.org/columns/straight-paths/better-than-before/ . Accessed on May 8, 2020.
22. John Calvin, *Commentary on the Book of Psalms, Vol. III*, trans. James Anderson (Grand Rapids: Wm. B. Eerdmans Publishing Company, 1949), 480.
23. As quoted in: Lee Strobel, *The Case for Miracles: A Journalist Investigates Evidence for the Supernatural* (Grand Rapids: Zondervan, 2018), 222.
24. I've heard the analogies about the operating room and Einstein elsewhere but can't recall the original sources. I also don't know the original source for Evelyn Underhill quote.
25. Max Lucado, *You'll Get Through This: Hope and Help For Your Turbulent Times* (Nashville: Thomas Nelson, 2013), 105.
26. You can read more about this study at: https://news.vanderbilt.edu/2017/05/31/worship-is-good-for-your-health-vanderbilt-study/
27. Lee Strobel, *The Case for Miracles: A Journalist Investigates Evidence for the Supernatural* (Grand Rapids: Zondervan, 2018), 231-232.
28. Max Lucado, *God Came Near: God's Perfect Gift* (Nashville: Thomas Nelson, 2004), 113.
29. Ben Parr, *Captivology: The Science of Capturing People's Attention* (New York: HarperOne, 2015), 133-134.
30. Max Lucado, *You'll Get Through This: Hope and Help For Your Turbulent Times* (Nashville: Thomas Nelson, 2013), 137.
31. Jud Wilhite, *The God of Yes: How Faith Makes All Things New* (New York: Faith Words, 2014), 162.
32. Francis Chan and Preston Sprinkle, *Erasing Hell: What God Said About Eternity, And The Things We Made Up* (Colorado Springs: David C Cook, 2011), 140-141.
33. Tim Cantopher, *Overcoming Stress: Advice for People Who Gives Too Much* (Louisville: Westminster John Knox Press, 2015), 1.
34. David Helm, *Expository Preaching: How We Speak God's Word Today* (Wheaton: Crossway, 2014), 70.
35. John Calvin, *Commentary on the Catholic Epistles*, trans. & ed. John Owen (Wm. B. Eerdmans Publishing Company: Grand Rapids, 1948), 239.
36. John Calvin, *Commentary on the Catholic Epistles*, trans. & ed. John Owen (Grand Rapids: Wm. B. Eerdmans Publishing Company, 1948), 239.

REFERENCES AND NOTES

37. Viktor Frankl, *Man's Search for Meaning*, trans. Ilse Lasch (Boston: Beacon Press, 1959), 60.
38. Brother Lawrence, *The Practice of the Presence of God* (Grand Rapids: Spire,1967), 70-71
39. As quoted in: John C. Lennox, *Where is God in a Coronavirus World?* (The Good Book Company, 2020), 62.
40. Andrew Murray, *With Christ in the School of Prayer* (Springdale: Whitaker House, 1981), 161.
41. Viktor Frankl, *Man's Search for Meaning*, trans. Ilse Lasch (Boston: Beacon Press, 1959), 44-45.
42. Daniel Goleman, *Emotional Intelligence: With it can matter more than IQ* (New York: Bantam, 1995), 240.
43. Max Lucado, *Wild Grace: What happens when grace happens* (Nashville: Thomas Nelson, 2012), 79.
44. As quoted in: Timothy Keller with Kathy Keller, *The Meaning of Marriage: Facing the Complexities of Commitment with the Wisdom of God* (New York: Dutton, 2011), 93.
45. This is a quote from chapter seven in Haidt's book *The Happiness Hypothesis: Finding Modern Truth in Ancient Wisdom* (New York: Basic Books, 2006). I haven't read it but have seen it used in various contexts.
46. Craig Groeschel, *Altar Ego: Becoming who God says you are* (Grand Rapids: Zondervan, 2013), 189-190.
47. Rebecca Konynkyk DeYoung, *Glittering Vices: A New Look at the Seven Deadly Sins* (New York: Rowman and Littlefield, 2000), 41.
48. Alain de Bottom, *Status Anxiety* (New York: Penguin, 2004), 3.
49. As quoted in "Facebook is a bummer, study says" by Geoffrey Mohan in The Los Angeles Times. Accessed at: https://www.latimes.com/science/la-xpm-2013-aug-14-la-sci-sn-facebook-bummer-20130814-story.html . Posted on August 14, 2013.
50. "The agony of Instagram" by Alex Williams was posted at *The New York Times* on December 13, 2013. You can access it here: https://www.nytimes.com/2013/12/15/fashion/instagram.html
51. Bob Russell with Rusty Russell, *Money: A User's Manual* (Sisters, OR: Multnomah, 1997), 69.
52. Francis Chan, *Forgotten God: Reversing our Tragic Neglect of the Holy Spirit* (Colorado Springs: David C Cook, 2009), 107.
53. Max Lucado, *You'll Get Through This: Hope and Help For Your Turbulent Times* (Nashville: Thomas Nelson, 2013), 97.
54. In John's Gospel the Holy Spirit is called Comforter four times (Greek: *Parakletos*). It is a word that is also translated as Advocate, Counselor or Helper. See John 14:16, 14:26, 15:26; 16:7.
55. Thomas More, *Utopia*, ed. G.M. Logan, trans. R. M. Adams (W.W. Norton and Company, 1975), 36.
56. A version of this story is told in: Tony Campolo, *Let Me Tell You A Story: Life Lessons from Unexpected Places and Unlikely People* (Nashville: Thomas Nelson, 2000), 201.

REFERENCES AND NOTES

57. As quoted in: *Hearts on Fire: Praying with Jesuits*, ed. Michael Harter (St. Louis: The Institute of Jesuit Sources, 1993), 73.
58. As quoted in: Kyle Idleman, *The End of Me: Where Real Life in the Upside-Down Ways of Jesus Begins* (David C Cook: Colorado Springs, 2015), 184.
59. John Piper, *Expository Exultation: Christian Preaching as Worship* (Wheaton: Crossway, 2018), 17.
60. As told in: Max Lucado, *3:16 – The Numbers of Hope* (Nashville: Thomas Nelson, 2007), 67-68.
61. Leonard Sweet and Frank Viola, *Jesus Speaks: Learning to Recognize and Respond to the Lord's Voice* (Nashville: Thomas Nelson, 2016), xiii-xiv.
62. Larry Osborne, *Sticky Leaders* (Grand Rapids: Zondervan, 2016), 23-24.)
63. Leonard Sweet & Frank Viola, *Jesus Speaks: Learning to Recognize & Respond to The Lord's Voice* (Nashville: W Publishing, 2016), p. 181-2.
64. Margaret Feinberg, *Fight Back with Joy* (Brentwood: Worthy, 2015), 26-28.
65. I heard this story from "Pastor Mark" on YouTube at https://www.youtube.com/watch?v=i0n009K49HU. Posted January 23, 2018.
66. Max Lucado, *3:16 – The Numbers of Hope* (Nashville: Thomas Nelson, 2007), 70.

ABOUT MATTHEW RUTTAN

Matthew Ruttan writes the "Up!" daily devotional, has been married to Laura since 2001, and is raising three children who have great questions. He is a servant of Jesus who loves studying the Bible, holds a Master of Divinity degree from Knox College (2008, Gold Medal, University of Toronto), has pastored Westminster Church in Barrie, Canada since 2008, won 'best blog' by the Canadian Church Press in 2015, and has had articles published by The Toronto Star, The Gospel Coalition Canada, and The Christian Courier. He grew up playing hockey in Muskoka, playing in a rock band in Toronto, has worked at the Ontario legislature, and has been getting more involved in the fight against human trafficking. He loves it when people discover and live out a powerful faith in practical ways each and every day.

Learn, watch or hear more at MatthewRuttan.com or TheUpDevo.com.

facebook.com/MatthewRuttanUp
twitter.com/theupdevo
instagram.com/theupdevo

Manufactured by Amazon.ca
Bolton, ON